GCSE in a wee

Biology

Jim Sharpe and Joanna Whitehead,
Abbey Tutorial College
Series Editor: Kevin Byrne

Where to find the information you need

Letts Educational
Aldine Place
London W12 8AW
Tel: 0181 740 2266
Fax: 0181 743 8451
e-mail: mail@lettsed.co.uk
website: http://www.lettsed.co.uk

First published 1998
Reprinted 1998, 1999 (three times)

Text © Jim Sharpe and Joanna Whitehead 1998
Design and illustration ©: (Letts Educational) Ltd 1998

British Library Cataloguing in Publication Data
A CIP record for this book is available from the British Library.

ISBN 1 85758 6956

Editorial, design and production by Hart McLeod, Cambridge

Printed in Great Britain by Ashford Colour Press

Letts Educational is the trading name of Letts Educational Ltd, a division of Granada Learning Ltd. Part of the Granada Media Group.

Cells and the movement of molecules

Test your knowledge

10 minutes

1 All living things move, respire, show sensitivity, grow, _reproduce_ , excrete and have nutrition.

2 The basic unit of any living organism is the _cell_ .

3 There are two main types of cell: animal cells and _plant_ cells.

4 A plant cell contains chloroplasts which contain a green pigment called _chlorophyl_ .

5 The lungs take in _oxygen_ and give out carbon dioxide.

6 The roots absorb water and _minerals_ into the plant.

7 A sperm cell has a _tail_ to swim towards the egg cell.

8 _Diffusion_ is the movement of molecules from a high concentration to a low concentration.

9 The movement of water molecules from a weak solution to a stronger solution across a semi-_permeable_ membrane is called osmosis.

10 _Active_ transport requires energy whereas passive transport does not require energy.

If you got them all right, skip to page 6

Cells and the movement of molecules

Improve your knowledge

30 minutes

1. All living things (animals/plants) do these seven things: this can be remembered as **MRS GREN**.

   Each letter represents a process. **M**ovement, **R**espiration, show **S**ensitivity, **G**rowth, **R**eproduction, **E**xcretion and **N**utrition.

2. Groups of **cells** of the same type are called **tissues**. Tissues that work together to perform a function (job) are called **organs**. An **organism** can either be made of one cell or even millions of cells, e.g. a bacterium or an oak tree.

   A **light microscope** is used to study cells because it magnifies them (i.e. makes them bigger). Learn how to label a diagram of a microscope with the following labels: eyepiece lens, focusing knob, handle, (low and high power) objective lens, stage, mirror and stage clips.

3. There are two main types of cell: an animal and a plant cell.

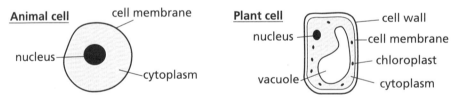

4. Learn the structure and function of each part of a plant cell:

   Nucleus controls the cell.

   Cell membrane allows certain substances into and out of the cell.

   Cytoplasm is where chemical reactions take place and is the liquid part of the cell.

   Cell wall holds up (supports) the plant and is made of cellulose.

   Vacuole stores the sugar solution.

   Chloroplasts contain the green pigment chlorophyll, which captures the sunlight for photosynthesis.

5 Each organ in animals has a particular function:

Brain controls the body.

Stomach digests food.

Small intestine digests and absorbs food into the bloodstream.

Large intestine absorbs water from food and stores the faeces.

Lungs take in oxygen (air) and get rid of carbon dioxide.

Heart pumps blood around the body.

Kidneys remove poisonous waste substances and control the amount of water in the body.

Testes produce the male sex cells (sperm) for reproduction.

Ovaries produce the female sex cells (egg cells or ova) for reproduction.

6 Each organ in plants has a particular function:

Flower helps to bring about pollination and produces seeds for reproduction.

Leaves photosynthesise to make food (starch) using sunlight.

Roots absorb water and minerals from the soil.

7 There are some cells in animals and plants which are **specialised** to perform a particular job (function).

In animals

Sperm cell
It has a long tail to swim to the ovum for fertilisation. The head contains genetic material that will decide your characteristics.

Nerve cell (neurone)
It has a long axon to carry messages (as electrical impulses) around the body.

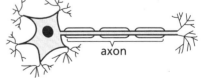

axon

Red blood cell
It does not contain a nucleus, allowing extra space for oxygen-carrying haemoglobin. Its shape helps it to take up oxygen and makes passing along narrow blood vessels easier.

surface view   side view

3

In plants

Palisade mesophyll cell
It has many chloroplasts which are needed
for photosynthesis.

Root hair cell
It has a large surface area to absorb
water and dissolved minerals.

8 Molecules always spread themselves out evenly to fill all the available space. Molecules move from a region where there are a lot of them (i.e. concentrated) until the concentration becomes the same. This is called **diffusion**. The cell membrane is **semi-permeable** i.e. small molecules like water can pass through easily and larger molecules like proteins cannot pass through easily. Diffusion depends on temperature, pressure, concentration gradient, surface area and thickness of the membrane.

9 **Osmosis** is the diffusion of water. It is the movement of water molecules from a weak solution to a strong solution across a semi-permeable membrane, e.g. water moves from the soil (weak solution) into the root hair cells (strong solution) by osmosis. In plant cells, when the cell is full of water, it is said to be **turgid**. If the cell loses water, it is said to be **flaccid**. When a plant cell is placed in a more concentrated solution, its cytoplasm shrinks away from the cell wall. The cell is said to be **plasmolysed**.

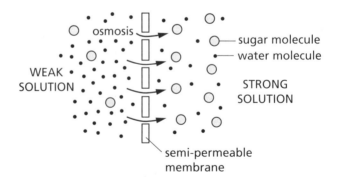

10 **Passive transport** does not require the cells to use energy and molecules move from a high concentration to a low concentration, e.g. diffusion.

Active transport requires energy and molecules can move from a low concentration to a high concentration.

Check list

Are you sure you understand these key terms?

cell / tissue / organ / specialised / diffusion / semi-permeable / osmosis / turgid / flaccid / plasmolysed / active transport / passive transport

✓ *Now learn how to use your knowledge*

Cells and the movement of molecules

Use your knowledge

 cell A   cell B   cell C

1 Name three differences between cell A and cell B.

Cell A has chloroplasts, a vacuole + a cell wall which aren't in cell B

Hint 1

2 What is the function of cell A and how is it well suited for its function?

To make starch, it has chloroplasts in for photosynthesis

Hint 2

3 In which layer of the leaf is cell A found?

Palisade – upper layer

Hint 3

4 How is water taken into cell C?

Through osmosis

Hint 4

5 Cell A is placed in a very concentrated sugar solution. The diagram shows what you would observe. How do we describe this cell?

Plasmolysed.

Hints 5/6

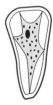

✓ *Hints and answers follow*

Cells and the movement of molecules

1 What structures can you see in cell A compared with cell B?

2 Why are there many chloroplasts containing chlorophyll?

3 Is it the upper or lower surface of the leaf?

4 What is the process called when water goes from a weak to a strong solution?

5 Look, the cytoplasm has shrunk away! What is this called?

6 Look at point 9 of *Improve your knowledge*.

Nutrition

Test your knowledge

10 minutes

1 A balanced diet for humans includes proteins, <u>Carbohydrates</u> and lipids. _____ is a disease caused by too little protein in their diet.

2 When <u>Benedicts</u> solution is used to test food, it turns <u>brick</u> <u>red</u> in colour if simple sugars are present.

3 Digestion is the breakdown of large <u>insoluble</u> molecules into <u>smaller</u> soluble molecules.

4 After chewing in the mouth, food passes down the <u>Oesophagus</u> to the stomach by the process of <u>peristalsis</u>. The partly digested food then enters the <u>small</u> <u>intestine</u>.

5 Our bodies digest the food we eat in two ways, by <u>Mechanical</u> and <u>Chemical</u> digestion.

6 Enzymes <u>increase</u> the speed of chemical reactions in the body. For example, <u>protease</u> break down proteins to amino acids.

7 The wall of the small intestine is folded to form thousands of <u>villi</u> which increase the surface area to absorb food. Each one of these contains numerous <u>capillaries</u> to carry food to the liver.

8 Some of the food absorbed after digestion is used in <u>respiration</u> to release energy. The rest of this food is used in <u>assimilation</u> to build up the structures of the body.

Answers

1 carbohydrates / Kwashiorkor
2 Benedict's / brick red **3** insoluble / smaller
4 oesophagus / peristalsis / small intestine
5 mechanical / chemical **6** increase /
proteases **7** villi / capillaries/blood vessels
8 respiration / assimilation

If you got them all right, skip to page 13

Nutrition

30 minutes

1 The table below shows the different food groups (or nutrients) needed. A **balanced diet** has all these food groups in the right amounts.

Food group	Good sources	Uses	Effect if not eaten in diet (deficiency disease)
Proteins	Eggs, meat	Muscles, enzymes Energy supply	*Kwashiorkor* – bloated belly, slow brain development
Lipids (fats and oils)	Butter, milk	Energy store Heat insulation	
Carbohydrates (sugars)	Potatoes, pasta	Energy supply Cell structure	
Vitamin C	Citrus fruit (e.g. oranges), milk	Repair of damaged tissues Healthy teeth and gums	*Scurvy* – poor healing of wounds, bleeding of gums
Vitamin D	Butter, egg yolk	Calcium depositing in bones	*Rickets* – weak and/or deformed bones
Calcium	Milk and cheese	Major part of teeth and bones	Fragile teeth and bones
Iron	Liver, egg yolk	Haemoglobin in red blood cells	*Anaemia* – lack of red blood cells
Fibre	Fresh vegetables	Movement of food through the gut	
Water	Drinking, fruit and vegetables	Animal bodies are over 75% water	

2 Chemical tests are used to see which type of carbohydrates different foods contain.

What are you testing for?	Chemical test used on food	Result if carbohydrate is present
Simple (reducing) sugars	Add blue Benedict's solution to food and warm	Solution turns brick red in colour
Starch (complex sugar)	Add brown iodine solution to food	Solution turns blue/black in colour

3 Digestion is the breakdown of the large, **insoluble** molecules in food into smaller, soluble molecules so they can then be absorbed across the cells of the gut into the body:

a) Carbohydrates are broken down into simple sugars.

b) Proteins are broken down into amino acids.

c) Lipids are broken down into fatty acids and glycerol.

4 The digestive system (alimentary canal/gut) breaks down the food ingested (taken in) and egests (removes) any indigestible material (e.g. fibre). The diagram below shows the layout of the human gut.

The human digestive system

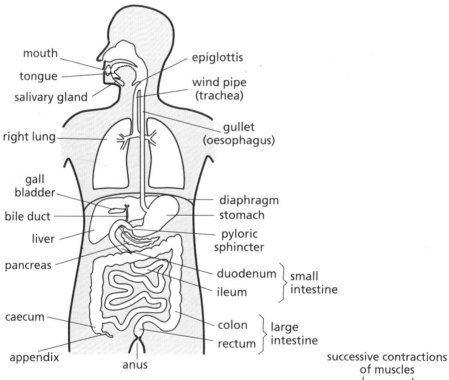

Peristalsis is the way food is moved along the gut. Antagonistic (opposing) muscles in the wall of the gut contract behind the food, squeezing it along.

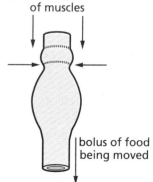

5 Food is digested in two ways:

   a) **Mechanical digestion** – Teeth and churning by the muscles of the stomach break food into small pieces, making chemical digestion easier.

   b) **Chemical digestion** – Enzymes secreted by cells and organs of the digestive system break down large food molecules.

6 Enzymes are biological catalysts – speeding up the chemical reactions without being changed themselves. There are three main types of enzymes:

   a) **Proteases** – hydrolyse (change chemically) proteins to amino acids.

   b) **Lipases** – hydrolyse lipids to fatty acids and glycerol.

   c) **Carbohydrases** – hydrolyse complex sugars to simple sugars. For example, **amylase** secreted in the mouth hydrolyses starch (complex sugar) to maltose (simple sugar).

7 The small intestine is well suited to carry out its job of absorbing digested food into the blood:

   a) Thousands of finger-like projections called **villi** (*singular* **villus**) project into the cavity of the intestine. This means that there is a very large surface area for absorption.

   b) Each villus contains numerous blood capillaries for transporting absorbed food to the liver.

   c) The wall of each villus is only one cell thick, so there is only a short distance for the food to travel into the blood.

A longitudinal section of a villus in the small intestine

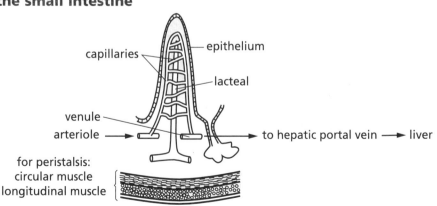

8 The small, soluble molecules absorbed at the small intestine are carried to the liver in the hepatic portal vein. Some of these are built back up into larger molecules in a process called **assimilation**.

Check list

Are you sure that you understand the following key terms?

balanced diet / Benedict's and iodine test / soluble / insoluble / peristalsis / chemical and mechanical digestion / enzymes / villi / assimilation

Now learn how to use your knowledge

Nutrition

Use your knowledge

20 minutes

The table below shows four different snacks and statements relevant to different food groups on the right.

Meal	Statement
A) Scrambled eggs on toast	a) Stops the disease scurvy
B) Glass of milk	b) Produces healthy teeth and bones
C) Spaghetti	c) Body building and provides iron
D) Glass of orange juice	d) Good energy food

1 Pair up each of the meals above with the most appropriate statement.

Hint 1

A) __C__ B) __b__ C) __d__ D) __a__

2 Explain how a group of students could find out whether the four meals above contain starch or simple sugars.

Hints 2/3

Starch/iodine test, benedicts test.

3 People who do a lot of physical exercise often believe that they need a diet containing large amounts of protein. Suggest why this belief may be wrong.

Hint 4

Carbohydrates provide energy.

4 In the last century, sailors on long sea journeys often suffered from bleeding gums and found injuries, such as cuts, didn't heal properly. What was the cause of the sailors' illness and suggest what they could have done to improve their health?

Hint 5

lack of vitamin C / eat fresh fruit

✓ *Hints and answers follow*

Nutrition

Hints

1 Think about the major food groups found in each of the meals.

2 There are two different solutions needed for these two tests.

3 What temperatures do the two tests have to be carried out at?

4 To do a lot of exercise you need energy. Energy comes from respiration. Which food group is the most important for respiration?

5 Which food group is needed for repair of damaged tissues and healthy teeth and gums?

Answers

1 A) c B) b C) d D) a **2** starch-iodine test / simple sugar-Benedict's test **3** diet should contain a large amount of carbohydrate to provide the energy needed (through respiration) **4** lack of vitamin C (scurvy) / eaten citrus fruit

Breathing and respiration

Test your knowledge

10 minutes

1 Breathing is the process of taking in oxygen and getting rid of ___Carbon___ ___dioxide___ using the ribs and ___diaphragm___

2 Air passes through the nose or mouth, down the ___trachea___, through the bronchi, the ___bronchiles___ and into the alveoli.

3 Alveoli have thin walls and a good blood supply for rapid ___diffusion___.

4 When we inhale, the rib cage moves upwards and ___out___ and the diaphragm ___flattens___.

5 Exhaled air contains more ___carbon___ ___dioxide___ and is warmer and ___wetter___ than inhaled air.

6 Aerobic respiration needs ___oxygen___.

7 After strenuous exercise, more oxygen is required to break down ___lactic___ ___acid___ into harmless substances. This is called ___oxygen___ ___debt___.

8 Smoking contains many harmful substances like tar, carbon monoxide and ___nicotine___.

Answers

1 carbon dioxide / diaphragm **2** trachea / bronchioles **3** diffusion **4** outwards / flattens **5** carbon dioxide / wetter **6** oxygen **7** lactic acid / oxygen debt **8** nicotine

If you got them all right, skip to page 19

Breathing and respiration

30 minutes

1 **Breathing** is the process of taking oxygen into the lungs and giving out carbon dioxide using the ribs and diaphragm. Breathing takes place in the lungs, which are found in the thorax (chest).

2 Learn how to label the structure of the thorax:

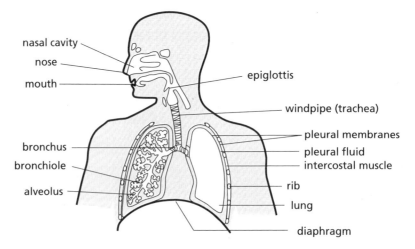

The air passes into our nose or mouth, down the **trachea** (windpipe) and this splits into two **bronchi** (*singular* **bronchus**). These divide into smaller tubes (**bronchioles**), which pass to the air sacs (**alveoli**).

The trachea and bronchi are kept open by rings of **cartilage**. The **epiglottis** stops food entering the trachea when we swallow. The trachea, bronchi and bronchioles have **ciliated** cells (i.e. with tiny hairs), which produce mucus. The mucus is sticky to trap bacteria and dirt and is swept by the cilia to the top of the trachea.

3 **Gaseous exchange** takes place between the alveoli and the blood capillaries. The alveoli are specialised for gaseous exchange because they have very thin walls and have a very good blood supply. There are 350 million alveoli, which make a very large surface area. This speeds up the diffusion of gases.

This diagram shows how oxygen diffuses from the alveoli into the blood capillary and carbon dioxide diffuses from the blood capillary into the alveoli.

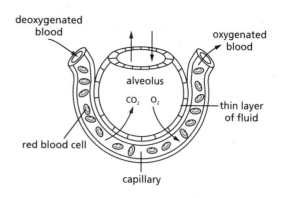

4 Air which enters the lungs is called **inhaled** air and air which leaves the lungs is called **exhaled** air. When we inhale, the diaphragm muscle flattens and the ribs are moved upwards and outwards by **intercostal muscles**. The volume of the thorax **expands** and lowers the **pressure**. Therefore, air rushes in. The opposite happens when we exhale.

A model of how we breathe can be shown using a bell jar :

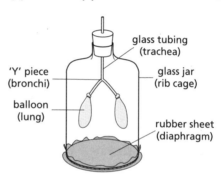

5 Compare the differences between inhaled and exhaled air in the table shown below:

	Inhaled air	**Exhaled air**
Oxygen	21%	16%
Carbon dioxide	0.04%	4%
Water vapour	Amount of water in the air	Saturated
Nitrogen	79%	79%

6 **Respiration** is the process which makes energy for living things. Respiration with oxygen is called **aerobic** respiration and respiration without oxygen is called **anaerobic** respiration.

a) **Aerobic respiration**

glucose + oxygen ⟶ **ENERGY** + carbon dioxide + water

b) **Anaerobic respiration**

In animal cells (muscles):

glucose $\longrightarrow$ **ENERGY** + lactic acid

In yeast cells:

glucose $\longrightarrow$ **ENERGY** + ethanol + carbon dioxide

Less energy is produced in anaerobic respiration compared with aerobic respiration.

7 During strenuous exercise, our muscles need more oxygen than we can breathe in. Therefore, we produce lactic acid by anaerobic respiration which builds up during exercise. Lactic acid causes our muscles to ache and it is a mild poison. We take in oxygen after exercise to break down the lactic acid into harmless substances and this is known as the **oxygen debt**.

Exercise also increases the heart rate so that more blood with oxygen is carried to respiring tissues. Caffeine also increases the heart rate. The fitter the person, the quicker the rate of recovery to the normal heart rate – on average about 70 beats per minute.

8 **Smoking** causes damage to the lungs because it contains tar, which stops cilia working properly. Two other harmful substances are also released from cigarettes – these are carbon monoxide and nicotine. Carbon monoxide prevents as much oxygen being carried around the blood. Nicotine stimulates nerve impulses and is addictive. Diseases caused by smoking include bronchitis, lung cancer and emphysema. Babies born to women who smoke are often smaller than average and there is an increased chance of premature birth and in some cases, death.

Check list

Are you sure you understand these key terms?

breathing / bronchi / alveoli / inhaled / exhaled / aerobic and anaerobic respiration / oxygen debt / smoking

✓ *Now learn how to use your knowledge*

20 minutes

Use your knowledge

The diagram shows the section of the thorax.

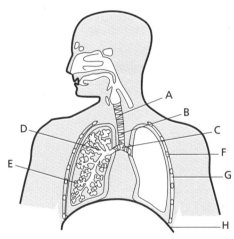

1 Name the parts labelled A to H.

(Hint 1)

A _trachea_   C _broncus_   E _alveoli_   G _Rib_

B _Cartildge_   D _bronciole_   F _intercostal Muscle_   H _diaphragm_

2 Explain how air enters the lungs.

(Hint 2)

_____

_____

3 Complete the table below to show the differences between inhaled and exhaled air:

(Hint 3)

	Inhaled air	Exhaled air
Oxygen	A _21 %_	16%
Nitrogen	79%	B _79%_
Carbon dioxide	C _0.04%_	4%

4 What process is the oxygen needed for? Hints 4/5

Respiration.

The graph below shows the breathing rate of Sarah before and after exercise.

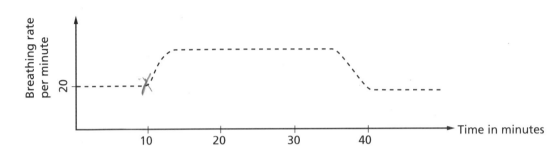

5 Mark on the diagram the point at which Sarah starts to exercise. Hint 6

6 What is the normal breathing rate for Sarah? Hint 7

20 breaths per minute

7 Explain why Sarah's breathing rate increases during exercise. Hint 8

More O₂ is needed for respiration + to provide energy for muscle contraction.

8 During the exercise, Sarah's muscles begin to ache. What is the chemical called which causes this effect? Hint 9

Lactic acid.

9 Why has this chemical been produced? Hint 10

lack of oxygen to the muscles.

✓ *Hints and answers follow*

Breathing and respiration

Hints

1 Learn this – look at diagram in point 2 of *Improve your knowledge*.

2 Learn this – look at number 4 in *Improve your knowledge*.

3 Learn this – look at number 5 in *Improve your knowledge*.

4 Oxygen is needed for the process to make energy.
    What is this called?

5 Look at number 6 in *Improve your knowledge*.

6 At which point does the breathing rate increase?

7 What was the breathing rate before it increased?

8 What gas is taken in by breathing, that is used for respiration?

9 Learn this – look at part (b), number 6 in *Improve your knowledge*.

10 What is there a lack of?

Answers

1 A – trachea / B – cartilage / C – bronchus / D – bronchiole / E – alveolus / F – rib / G – intercostal muscle / H – diaphragm 2 intercostal muscles and diaphragm contract (flatten). The volume of the thorax increases and the pressure decreases and air rushes in 3 A – 21% / B – 79% / C – 0.04% 4 respiration 5 point at 10 mins 6 20 breaths per minute 7 more oxygen is needed for the process of respiration, to provide energy for muscular contraction 8 lactic acid 9 lack of oxygen to the muscles, called oxygen debt

Blood and circulation

Test your knowledge

10 minutes

1 The blood has three major functions. These are transport, _defence_ and _clotting_ .

2 Blood is made up of two parts: _plasma_ , a straw-coloured liquid and _cells_ , which make up the solid part.

3 The _____ shape of red blood cells means that they have a large _surface_ _area_ to absorb _oxygen_ .

4 _Arteries_ carry blood away from the heart. Their walls have an elastic layer and a _muscle_ layer because of the high pressure.

5 Mammals have a double circulatory system. The _Right_ side pumps blood to the lungs and the left side pumps blood around the _body_ .

6 The _vena_ _cava_ blood vessel carries blood from the body to the right side of the heart. The blood is then pumped from the heart to the _lungs_ via the pulmonary artery.

7 Each side of the heart has two halves. The top halves are called _atria_ and the bottom halves are called _ventricles_ .

Answers

If you got them all right, skip to page 26

Blood and circulation

Improve your knowledge

30 minutes

1. The blood has three important functions:
   a) **Transport** of oxygen, food, wastes (carbon dioxide and urea), hormones and heat.
   b) **Fighting infection** against invading organisms (e.g. bacteria and viruses) which cause disease and infection.
   c) **Blood clotting** to stop the loss of blood at wounds.

2. Blood is made up of two parts:
   a) **Plasma** (straw-coloured liquid) – 90% water and 10% dissolved substances.
   b) **Cells** (non-liquid part) – red blood cells, white blood cells and platelets.

3. You must understand that the appearance of blood cells directly relates to their job within the blood:

Cell	Function	Appearance	Explanation of adaptations
Red blood cells	Transport of oxygen from lungs to respiring cells	Biconcave with no nucleus Contain the red pigment haemoglobin	Cells have a larger surface area to absorb O_2 Chemical to which O_2 easily attaches
White blood cells	Fighting disease and infection by attacking organisms invading the body	Large cells with different shaped nuclei	Large size: helps cells attack invading organisms
Platelets	Prevent blood loss during injury	Fragments of whole cells	Able to stick together to form a plug Produce enzymes to clot blood (make solid 'lumps')

4 **Blood vessels** are branched tubes transporting blood to every part of the body. Their appearance varies depending on the job they perform:

Blood vessel	Function	Appearance	Explanation of adaptations
Arteries	Carry blood away from the heart under high pressure Mainly carry blood with oxygen in (oxygenated)	Walls have elastic outer layer and thicker muscle layer	Elastic and muscle layers: absorb pressure produced by heart Muscle layer: squeeze blood to help move it along
Capillaries	Carry blood from arteries to veins very slowly Allow oxygen and food to go into cells, and waste to be removed into the blood	Walls are very thin (one cell thick) and have holes (pores) in them	Thin walls: useful products and wastes only have a short distance to travel Pores: to allow fluid to leave blood
Veins	Carry blood back to the heart under low pressure Mainly carry blood which has lost its oxygen (deoxygenated)	Walls much thinner than arteries **Valves** present (flaps on the inside wall)	Valves: stop blood flowing backwards due to the low pressure

5 The blood is pumped around the body by the **heart**, found between the two lungs. It can be considered as two pumps joined together.

Double circulation of blood through the heart of a mammal

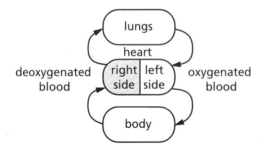

The two pumps **contract** (squeeze) at the same time. The blood passes through the heart twice before going back around the body – this is what is meant by a double circulatory system.

Look at the diagram above very carefully – the left- and right-hand side are reversed. The *right side of the heart* is on the left-hand side, and the *left side of the heart* is on the right-hand side. This may sound a little confusing, but it is because of the sides of the body that they are on.

6 It is important that you know about the following blood vessels:

Blood vessel	from the	to the
Vena cava	body	right side of the heart
Pulmonary artery	right side of the heart	lungs
Pulmonary vein	lungs	left side of the heart
Aorta	left side of the heart	body
Hepatic portal vein	small intestine	liver
Renal artery	aorta	kidneys
Renal vein	kidney	vena cava

7 The structure of the heart is divided into two halves. The top halves are thin-walled **atria**, and the bottom halves are thicker muscular-walled **ventricles**. Blood enters the atria first, which pumps the blood into the ventricles. The ventricles pump the blood out of the heart to the lungs and body. Ventricles have thicker muscular walls than the atria because they pump the blood a greater distance.

Structure of the heart

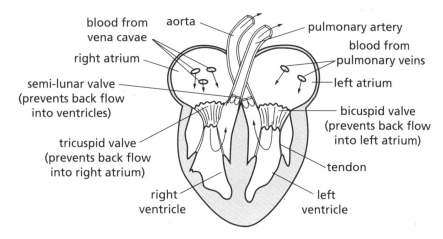

Check list

Are you sure that you understand the following key terms?

plasma / red blood cells / white blood cells / platelets / biconcave / blood vessels / arteries / capillaries / veins / atria / ventricles

 Now learn how to use your knowledge

Use your knowledge

20 minutes

These cells are taken from human blood.

cell A   cell B

1 State one function of cell A and one function of cell B.

CellA- transports oxygen

cell B- defends against infection

2 Identify and explain two visible features of cell A that help it perform its function.

Hint 1

Cell A- has no nucleus to increase volume

cell B-

3 This diagram shows a simplified heart with the main blood vessels.

Which of the blood vessels contains blood at the highest pressure?

2

Hints 2/3

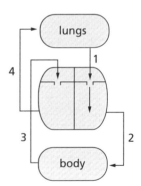

4 What is the name given to the largest pair of chambers in the heart? Explain how the appearance of the left-hand chamber relates to its function.

Ventricles- thick wall to pump blood round the body

✓ *Hints and answers follow*

Blood and circulation

1 Remember to compare structure to function. How is cell A different from a normal cell? These are the features that help it perform its function.

2 Think how blood pressure is produced – the blood vessel nearest where the blood pressure is produced must have the highest blood pressure.

3 The heart is simply a pump made up of muscle. Think where this chamber pumps the blood to and what this will do to the amount of muscle needed, compared with other chambers of the heart.

Answers

1 A – transport of oxygen / B – defence against infection **2** no nucleus – increases volume available to carry O_2 / biconcave shape – increases surface area to take up O_2 **3** 2/aorta **4** ventricles – thick muscular wall to pump the blood away from the heart around the body

Movement

1 The joints in the body are divided into two types: _fixed_ and moveable joints. There are two different types of moveable joints. The hip is an example of a _Socket_ and _ball_ joint, and the elbow is an example of a _hinge_ joint.

2 The upper bone in the arm, the _____ , is joined to the two lower bones, the radius and _____ , by a hinge joint.

3 Can you label the following diagram of an elbow hinge joint?

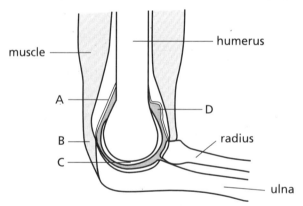

muscle

humerus

A

D

B

radius

C

ulna

4 Muscles work in pairs to bend (flex) and _straighten_ (extend) the arm. When the biceps muscle contracts the arm _flexes_ , and when the _triceps_ muscle contracts the arm extends.

5 Artificial joints are commonly used to replace damaged joints. For artificial joints to be a good replacement for a natural joint, they must be strong, _durable_ , _light_ and have friction-free surfaces.

Answers

1 fixed / ball / socket / hinge 2 humerus / ulna 3 A – synovial capsule / B – tendon / C – cartilage / D – synovial fluid 4 straighten / flexes / triceps 5 long-lived / light-weight

If you got them all right, skip to page 32

Movement

Improve your knowledge

30 minutes

1. Joints are the positions where bones are linked together. There are two types:

   a) **Fixed joints** – these are interlocking edges of bones, e.g. the bones in the vertebral column (backbone).

   b) **Moveable joints** – this is where bones are moving against each other. The two main types of moveable joint are:

      i) **ball and socket joints** – allow movement forwards, backwards and sideways, e.g. the hip joint

      ii) **hinge joints** – allow movement in only one plane. That is like the opening and closing of a door, e.g. the elbow or the knee.

2. The elbow hinge joint joins the upper arm bone – the **humerus**, to the lower arm bones – the **radius** and **ulna**. The ulna and radius can move around each other so that we can hold our hand palm up or palm down.

3. The diagram below shows the hinge joint in a human arm.

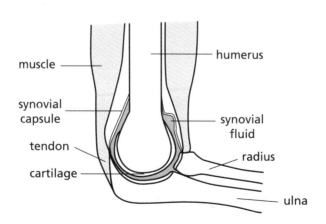

The following are the major components of a hinge joint:

Cartilage – smooth, rubbery protein which reduces the friction between bones as they move and rub against each other.

Synovial fluid – a thin layer of fluid which acts as a lubricant between bones, reducing friction.

Synovial capsule – a tough capsule enclosing and protecting the joint, which produces synovial fluid.

Ligaments – tough bands of elastic fibre holding the bones together.

Tendons – inelastic fibres attaching muscles to the bones.

4   The arm is moved by the two muscles shown in the diagram below.

a) **Biceps muscle** – its contraction **bends** (flexes) the arm at the elbow.

b) **Triceps muscle** – its contraction **straightens** (extends) the arm at the elbow.

Muscles work in pairs with each muscle having an opposite effect. For example, the contraction of the biceps will flex the arm, such as when we are lifting a drink from a table. However, to straighten the arm, and put the drink back on the table, the contraction of the triceps is needed to pull the contracted biceps back. Pairs of muscles working together are called **antagonistic muscles**.

The opposite effect of antagonistic muscles is shown in the diagram.

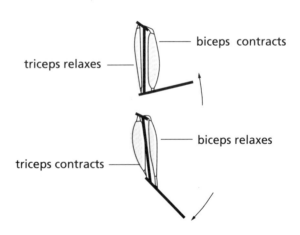

5 Damaged joints can be replaced with **artificial joints**. The most common joint replacement is the hip joint, particularly in people suffering from arthritis. The head of the bone (the femur) is replaced by a stainless steel 'ball' and the socket is replaced by a plastic 'cup'. The material used to make artificial joints must have the following characteristics:

- Strong

- Light-weight

- Long-lived

- Friction-free surfaces.

Check list

Are you sure that you understand the following key terms?

fixed joints / moveable joints / ball and socket joints / hinge joints / bones / antagonistic muscles / cartilage / synovial fluid / synovial capsule / ligaments / tendons / artificial joints

 Now learn how to use your knowledge

Movement

Use your knowledge

20 minutes

1 Describe how synovial fluid and cartilage reduce friction in joints. *Hint 1*

> Synovial fluid lubricates the joint + cartilage.
> Cartilage is smooth to reduce friction between
> the bones

2 Joints can become damaged with age or disease, e.g. osteo-arthritis where cartilage breaks down. They may be replaced by artificial joints. Suggest why osteo-arthritis causes considerable pain. *Hint 2*

> It causes stiffness and increases friction
> in the joints.

3 Artificial joints need to be strong, light-weight and long-lived. Suggest why you think each of these characteristics is important. *Hint 3*

_____

_____

4 Diagram of a labelled section through an elbow joint. *Hint 4*

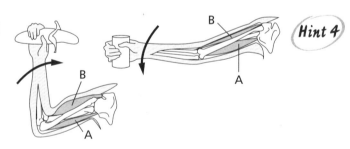

Explain how and why the movement of the elbow would be affected if muscle B became separated from the radius bone.

_____

_____

Hints and answers follow

Movement

Hints

1   In the diagram on page 28, part C is a liquid and part D is a rubbery
    coating to the bone.
    Think how these characteristics could reduce friction.

2   Think about the role of the cartilage in a joint and what the
    effect on the joint would be of removing it.

3   Consider what is involved in fitting an artificial joint and what
    happens to an artificial joint during its lifetime.

4   Muscles work in pairs because each one can only make the arm
    move in one direction. With only one muscle working on the arm,
    what is going to happen?

Answers

1 synovial fluid, an oily liquid, lubricates the joint, and cartilage, a smooth, rubbery protein
reduces friction between bones 2 joints lose shock absorbers and friction occurs between them,
wearing bone and causing pain 3 strong – stress body places on joints / light-weight – reduces
effort for muscles and bones – long-lived – prevent need for replacement 4 arm could extend,
but not flex – A extends arm, B needed for flexing (muscles work in antagonistic pairs)

Nerves, hormones and homeostasis

Test your knowledge

10 minutes

1 Living organisms detect changes in our environment called
Stimuli using special cells in our body called _receptors_ .

2 The central nervous system is made up of the brain and the
spinal cord .

3 The three neurones found in the reflex arc are called the sensory, relay
and _Motor_ neurones.

4 To allow more light into the eye, antagonistic muscles in the iris cause
the _pupil_ to expand.

5 If a person is short-sighted, they need to wear spectacles containing
a _concave_ lens.

6 Insulin is an example of a _hormone_ , which is produced in the
pancreas . It changes glucose into _glycogen_ in the liver.

7 _Homeostasis_ is the ability to maintain a constant internal
environment.

8 The kidneys control the amount of _water_ in the blood and
excrete _toxic_ waste substances.

9 If a person gets too hot, the blood vessels near the surface of the skin
dilate to allow heat to escape by _radiation_ .

If you got them all right, skip to page 38

Nerves, hormones and homeostasis

Improve your knowledge

30 minutes

1 Living organisms detect changes in their environment called **stimuli**, e.g. taste, touch, smell, light. **Receptors** are special cells that detect stimuli.

2 The nervous system has a control centre called the **central nervous system**, which is made up of the **brain** and the **spinal cord**. Nerves carry messages to and from the central nervous system.

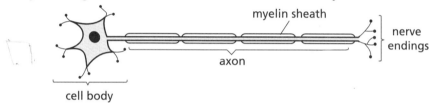

3 A **reflex action** is the automatic, rapid response to a stimulus. There are three nerves found in the reflex arc (the pathway) and these are called the sensory, relay and motor neurone. For example, if you put your finger into a hot Bunsen burner flame:

a) The stimulus (heat) is detected by a pain receptor in the skin.

b) The **sensory neurone** carries an impulse to the spinal cord.

c) The **relay neurone** carries the impulse to the **motor neurone**.

d) The motor neurone carries the impulse to a muscle in the arm.

e) The impulse reaches a muscle in your arm, which contracts, pulling the arm away from the Bunsen burner. The muscle is called the **effector**.

4 Learn the structure of the eye:

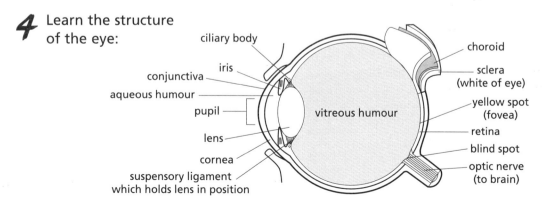

35

5 Humans are able to focus on objects by changing the shape of the lens. This is called **accommodation**.

To see a distant object, the lens has to be long and thin.
To see a near object, the lens has to be short and fat.

If a person is **short-sighted**, the light is focused **in front** of the retina. It can be corrected by wearing a **concave** lens, which will **diverge** (spread out) the light.

If a person is **long-sighted**, the light would focus **behind** the retina. It can be corrected by wearing a **convex** lens, which will **converge** (bring closer) the light.

6 Hormones are chemical messengers made in **endocrine glands** released directly into the bloodstream.

Hormone	Endocrine gland	Action of hormone
Insulin	Pancreas	Changes glucose into glycogen in liver
Adrenaline	Adrenal glands	Increases heart rate for fight or flight
Testosterone	Testes	Secondary sexual characteristics
Oestrogen	Ovary	Secondary sexual characteristics
Progesterone	Ovary	Maintains uterus lining and prevents ovulation

7 **Homeostasis** is the ability to maintain a constant internal environment, e.g. blood sugar level.

8 The kidneys control the volume of water in the blood and **excrete** poisonous waste substances (e.g. **urea**). Blood enters the kidneys through the **renal artery** and goes out through the **renal vein**. The kidneys act like complex filters and clean the blood by removing all of the urea and some of the salts and water in a healthy person. This is called **urine**. The **ureter** carries urine from the kidney to the **bladder**, which stores urine. Urine leaves the bladder through a tube called the **urethra** when the muscle relaxes.

9 The regulation of temperature in the body is called thermoregulation. The skin is the organ which regulates body temperature. Learn how to label the skin:

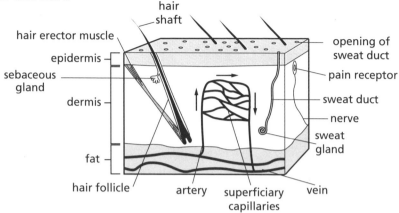

If a person gets too hot:

a) The sweat glands produce sweat, cooling the skin by evaporation.

b) The blood vessels near the surface of the skin get bigger. This is called **vasodilation**. This allows heat from the blood to escape by radiation.

c) The hair erector muscle relaxes so that the hairs lie flat against the skin.

If a person gets too cold:

a) The sweat glands do not produce sweat.

b) The blood vessels near the surface of the skin get smaller. This is called **vasoconstriction** and less heat escapes.

c) The hair erector muscle contracts so that the hair stands up. This traps a layer of air around the skin, which keeps us warm by insulation. In humans, this is called 'goose pimples'!

d) The muscles contract in a process called shivering, which keeps us warm.

e) There is a fatty layer in the skin, which keeps us warm (insulation).

Check list

Are you sure you understand the following key terms?

stimuli / receptors / central nervous system / reflex action / accommodation / endocrine gland / homeostasis / excrete / kidney failure / vasodilation / vasoconstriction

 Now learn how to use your knowledge

Nerves, hormones and homeostasis

Use your knowledge

20 minutes

1 Put the statements below in the correct sequence to explain how a reflex arc happens.

Hint 1

a) Pain is detected by pain receptors in the skin by the drawing pin in the foot.

b) The impulse reaches a muscle in your foot called an effector and pulls the foot away from the drawing pin.

c) The receptor starts an impulse in the sensory neurone.

d) The impulse passes from a relay neurone to the motor neurone.

2 What is the advantage of the reflex action?

Hint 2

_____

3 The pupils in our eyes also show a reflex action to light. Draw in the pupils in the diagrams below to show the appearance of the eyes.

Hint 3

dim light   bright light

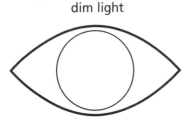   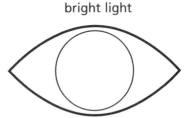

4 If a person is long-sighted, which lens is used to correct the sight and why?

Hints 4/5

_____

_____

38

5 Complete the table below:

Hint 6

Endocrine gland	Hormone	What the hormone does
Adrenal gland		Gets the body ready for action by increasing heart and breathing rate
	Insulin	Controls the amount of sugar in the body
Ovaries	Oestrogen and progesterone	
Testes		Controls secondary sexual characteristics

6 Urine can be tested to see if a person has diabetes or kidney damage. If they have diabetes, sugar will be present. If they have kidney damage, protein will be present. The urine of a normal person will contain water, salts and urea.

Look at the results below:

Name	Contents of urine
Michael	Water, salts, urea and sugar
Emma	Water, salts and urea
Maria	Water, salts, urea and protein

a) Which person is suffering from diabetes?

Hint 7

_____

b) Which person is suffering from kidney damage?

Hint 8

_____

Hints and answers follow

Nerves, hormones and homeostasis

Hints

1 Learn this – look at number 3 in *Improve your knowledge.*

2 Look at number 3 in *Improve your knowledge.*

3 The pupils get bigger and smaller in different lights. Draw the correct appearance of the pupil.

4 A short-sighted person needs the light rays to diverge (spread out) before entering the eye. Which lens diverges light?

5 Look at number 5 in *Improve your knowledge.*

6 Learn this – look at number 6 in *Improve your knowledge.*

7 Which person has sugar in their urine (diabetes)?

8 Which person has protein in their urine (kidney damage)?

Reproduction

Test your knowledge

10 minutes

1 The __Oviduct__ is the place where fertilisation takes place.

2 The __testes__ produce the sperm.

3 The fertilised egg is called a ~~zygote~~ *zygote*, which develops into the __embryo__ .

4 The foetus is joined to the mother by the __umbilical cord__ and __placenta__ . The foetus's and mother's blood __never__ mix.

5 Labour is the contraction of the __uterus__ wall and the baby is pushed out through the __vagina__ .

6 Contraception is used to prevent __pregnancy__ .

7 The menstrual cycle takes __28__ days.

8 The stamen is made up of the __anther__ and __filament__ .

9 __Pollination__ is the transfer of pollen from the anther to the stigma.

10 There are three methods of dispersing seeds. These are __Wind__ , self and __animal__ dispersal.

Answers

✔ *If you got them all right, skip to page 45*

Reproduction

Improve your knowledge

30 minutes

1 Learn the structure and function of the female reproductive system:

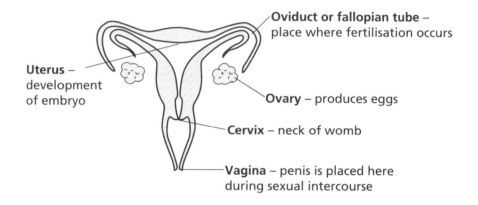

Uterus – development of embryo

Oviduct or fallopian tube – place where fertilisation occurs

Ovary – produces eggs

Cervix – neck of womb

Vagina – penis is placed here during sexual intercourse

2 Learn the structure and function of the male reproductive system:

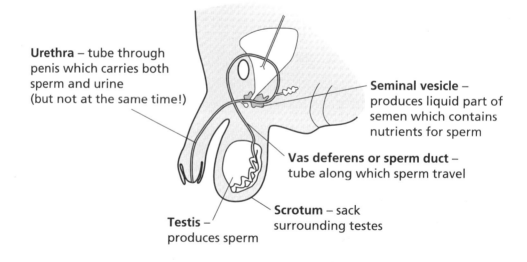

Urethra – tube through penis which carries both sperm and urine (but not at the same time!)

Seminal vesicle – produces liquid part of semen which contains nutrients for sperm

Vas deferens or sperm duct – tube along which sperm travel

Scrotum – sack surrounding testes

Testis – produces sperm

3 **Sexual intercourse** or **copulation** occurs when the penis is placed into the vagina. Millions of sperm are released (**ejaculation**) into the vagina and this increases the chances of the sperm reaching an egg. The sperm may penetrate the egg (**fertilisation**). The fertilised egg is called a **zygote** and continues to divide into an **embryo**. The embryo sinks into the uterus lining and this is called **implantation**. The woman is now **pregnant**.

4 The embryo grows into a **foetus** which looks like a miniature baby. The foetus is joined to the mother by the **placenta** and **umbilical cord**. The foetus obtains oxygen and food from the mother's blood and urea and carbon dioxide diffuses from the foetus's blood to the mother's blood. The mother's and foetus's blood **never** mix.

The baby is protected from knocks and bumps by **amniotic fluid** found in the **amniotic sac**. It takes nine months for the baby to develop and this is called the **gestation period**.

5 Birth is started off with the contraction of the muscles in the uterus and this is called **labour**. The baby is pushed out head first through the vagina. After a few minutes, the **after-birth** (placenta and umbilical cord) is pushed out.

6 Contraception is used to prevent pregnancy:

Men	Women
Condom	Contraceptive pill
Vasectomy	Coil (IUD)
	Cap (diaphragm)
	Female sterilisation

7 The **menstrual cycle** occurs in women from **puberty** (~ 13 yrs) to the **menopause** (40–50 yrs). The cycle takes ~ 28 days. An egg is released into the oviduct at ~ day 14. This is called **ovulation**. The egg moves down towards the uterus; a spongy layer, thickened with blood capillaries. If the egg is not fertilised, the uterus lining breaks down and blood flows out through the vagina. This is called **menstruation** or a **period** and lasts for ~ 5–7 days. To absorb the blood flow, a **sanitary towel** or **tampon** is used.

8 Learn the structure of the flower and what each part does:

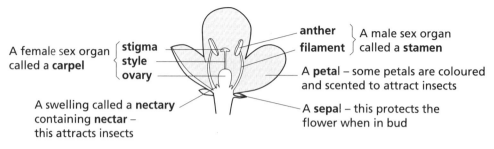

A female sex organ called a **carpel** { **stigma** **style** **ovary**

A swelling called a **nectary** containing **nectar** – this attracts insects

anther } A male sex organ called a **stamen**
filament

A **petal** – some petals are coloured and scented to attract insects

A **sepal** – this protects the flower when in bud

9 **Pollination** is the transfer of pollen from an anther to a stigma. Transfer in the same flower is called **self-pollination**. Transfer between different flowers is called **cross-pollination**. There are two types of cross-pollination – **wind** and **insect pollination**.

Insect pollination	Wind pollination
Brightly coloured and scented petals to attract insects	Dull coloured (usually green or brown) and no scent
Nectar produced	No nectar produced
Stamens and stigma found inside flower	Stamens long and stigmas long and feathery. Both hang outside the flower
Pollen grains are heavy with hooks	Pollen grains are light and smooth

10 After the seed has been formed, it needs to be **dispersed** so that it does not compete with the parent plant for light, water and nutrients.

a) self dispersal
   e.g. sweetpea

b) wind dispersal
   e.g.dandelion

c) animal dispersal
   e.g. burdock

Check list

Are you sure you understand these key terms?

ovary / testis / sexual intercourse / zygote / implantation / gestation period / labour / contraception / menstruation / pollination / dispersal

✓ *Now learn how to use your knowledge*

Reproduction

Use your knowledge

20 minutes

This diagram shows the female reproductive system.

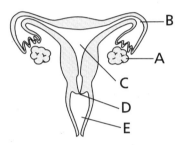

B
A
C
D
E

1 Name the parts labelled A to E.

Hint 1

A _Ovary_   C _uterus_   E _Vagina_

B _Oviduct_   D _cervix_

2 What is the job of the ovaries?

Hint 2

Produce the egg cells

3 If no fertilisation occurs, what happens to the uterus wall? What is this process called?

Hints 3/4

Uterus lining breaks down / menstruation

4 Explain why mothers should not drink or smoke during pregnancy.

Hints 5/6

Alcohol crosses the placenta to the baby & can cause brain damage. Smoking produces carbon monoxide which prevents haemoglobin from carrying oxygen.

5 How long is the gestation period for the human baby?

Hints 7/8

9 months

✔ *Hints and answers follow*

Reproduction

Hints

1 Learn this – look at number 1 in *Improve your knowledge*.

2 What do ovaries produce?

3 The uterus wall is no longer needed – what happens to it?

4 Look at number 7 in *Improve your knowledge*.

5 What harmful substances do cigarettes and alcohol contain?

6 How do nicotine and alcohol affect the development of the embryo?

7 How long is the time from conception to birth?

8 Look at number 4 in *Improve your knowledge*.

Answers

1 A – ovary / B – oviduct / C – uterus / D – cervix / E – vagina 2 produce the egg cells 3 the uterus lining breaks down / menstruation 4 alcohol crosses the placenta to the baby and can cause brain damage; smoking contains carbon monoxide, which prevents the haemoglobin from carrying oxygen, this causes the baby to be smaller and to have a greater chance of catching an infection 5 9 months

Genetics

10 minutes

1 Variation is controlled by two factors; _genes_ found on chromosomes, and _environment_ factors.

2 Characteristics are controlled by a _pair_ of genes called alleles. A recessive allele of a gene only controls the characteristics if the other allele of the gene is also _genotype_.

3 The way that an animal looks is its _phenotype_. The combination of different genes in the cells is known as the _genotype_.

4 In humans, the number of paired chromosomes is _46_, although gametes are haploid, having _23_ unpaired chromosomes.

5 The pair of sex chromosomes are either X or _Y_. For example, in humans, cells in a man have the genotype _XY_.

6 The following genetic diagram shows the cross between a brown-eyed father (Bb) and a blue-eyed mother. Brown (B) is dominant over blue (b).

a) Parents' phenotype   Brown eyes   ✗   Blue eyes

b) Parents' genotypes   Bb   ✗   _____

c) Possible gametes   ___ or ___   ✗   b or b

d) Offspring's genotype   Bb ____   ____ bb

e) Offspring's phenotype   Brown Brown   Blue Blue

7 Sickle cell disease is an inherited blood disease. It can be contracted through the harmful effects of an inherited _____ .

✔ *If you got them all right, skip to page 51*

Genetics

1 Every organism on Earth looks different from every other organism, even individuals of the same species are different. These differences in characteristics are known as **variation**.

Plant and animal characteristics are controlled by two factors:

a) **Genes** carry information to produce an individual's characteristics. They are found in the nucleus on **chromosomes**; thread-like structures made up of DNA and proteins. They occur in body cells as matching, or **homologous pairs**.

b) **Environment**. For example, imagine two plants with identical genes. If one of the plants is sheltered from wind, it will grow taller than a plant growing in an exposed, windy environment.

2 The two chromosomes of a homologous pair are matching. They have the same genes at the same positions. These pairs of genes on homologous chromosomes are called **alleles** and produce the same characteristic, e.g. eye colour. However, both genes may not produce the same eye colour; one may produce blue eyes and one brown eyes. Since people do not usually have one brown and one blue eye, one gene dominates over the other. **Dominant** genes always express themselves as a characteristic. **Recessive** genes only express themselves when the other gene in the allele pair is also recessive.

3 There are two ways in which we can describe an animal or plant.

a) The way it looks, e.g. eye colour – the **phenotype**.

b) The genes in the cell – the **genotype**.

Two people with brown eyes have the same phenotype, but they may have different genotypes. One may have two genes for brown eyes, the other may have one gene for brown eyes and one gene for blue eyes, but the gene for brown eyes is dominant.

4 Cells with the full number of paired chromosomes are said to be **diploid**. In humans the **diploid number is 46** (23 pairs of chromosomes).

In each pair one chromosome comes from the male parent and one from the female parent, when sperm and egg cells join in fertilisation. This means gametes are haploid, having half the full number of chromosomes, with no pairs. In humans, the **haploid number is 23**. This means the diploid number stays the same in every generation.

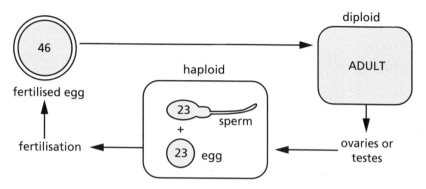

5 One of the 23 pairs of chromosomes is called **sex chromosomes**, because they control whether a fertilised egg becomes a male or female. Sex chromosomes are described by appearance and are either;

X chromosome (long) or **Y chromosome** (short).

Male diploid cells contain both an X and a Y chromosome – **XY**.
Female diploid cells contain two X chromosomes – **XX**.

Genetic diagrams show there is a 50% chance of a baby being a boy or a girl:

Phenotype:	Male			Female	
Genotype:	XY			XX	
Possible gametes:	Ⓧ	Ⓨ	fertilisation	Ⓧ	Ⓧ
Childrens' genotype:	XX	XX		XY	XY
Childrens' phenotype:	Female	Female		Male	Male

therefore 50% male and 50% female.

6 Genetic diagrams are used to predict the genotypes of the children from two parents. Letters are used to represent genes; the dominant gene is represented by a capital letter, e.g. 'B' (for brown eyes); and the recessive gene represented by 'b' (for blue eyes).

a) A person with blue eyes must have genotype bb.

b) A person with brown eyes can be genotype BB or Bb.

The diagram below shows a genetic diagram for a cross between a brown-eyed father and a blue-eyed mother.

	Father		**Mother**
a) Write down the parents' **phenotype**:	Brown eyes	×	Blue eyes
b) Write down the parents' **genotypes**:	Bb	×	bb
c) Write down the possible **gametes**: (eggs and sperm)	(B) or (b)	×	(b) or (b)
d) Draw in all the possible crosses: (i.e. **childrens' genotype**)	Bb Bb		bb bb
e) Write down the childrens' **phenotype**:	Brown Brown		Blue Blue

There is a 50% chance offspring are Bb (brown-eyed) and a 50% chance they are bb (blue-eyed).

An individual who has the same genes for a characteristic, e.g. BB or bb, is **homozygous**. An individual who has both the dominant and recessive gene, e.g. Bb, is **heterozygous**.

7 Some genes (dominant or recessive) produce harmful effects when inherited. For example, **sickle cell disease** is an inherited blood disease. Most people are homozygous (HH) for the dominant gene producing normal red blood cells. Sufferers are homozygous (hh) for the recessive gene producing abnormal shaped red blood cells (sickle shaped) reducing their ability to carry oxygen around the body.

Check list

Are you sure that you understand the following key terms?

variation / genes / chromosomes / alleles / homologous chromosomes / phenotype / genotype / inheritance / diploid / sex chromosomes / haploid / selective breeding

✓ *Now learn how to use your knowledge*

Genetics

20 minutes

	Male	Female
Parents' body cells:		
Gamete cells:		
	sperm	eggs
Child's body cells:		

1 In the spaces in the diagram above, fill in the number of chromosomes for each of the body cells.

Hint 1

2 Body cells are said to be diploid for chromosome number. What is the name given to the number of chromosomes in sperm and egg cells? _____

Hint 2

3 Explain the significance of the difference in the number of chromosomes in body cells compared with gamete cells.

Hint 3

_____

_____

_____

The diagram below shows the inheritance of eye colour in a family. The gene for brown eyes (B) is dominant over the gene for blue eyes (b):

	Father				Mother	
	Bb				Bb	
BB	bb		bb	Bb	
Ian	Colin	Cindy (brown)	Tracy	Justine	Lucie (blue)

4 What is Lucie's genotype for eye colour?

_____

Hint 4

5 Work out the two possible genotypes that Cindy has for eye colour.

_____

Hint 5

6 Explain how Ian and Justine have the same phenotype for eye colour but have different genotypes.

_____

_____

_____

Hint 6

7 Is it more likely that the next baby will be male than female? Explain your answer.

_____

Hint 7

A rare disease is carried on the same chromosome as the gene for blue eyes. If the gene for the disease is recessive:

8 Would the mother or the father suffer from the disease?

_____

_____

Hint 8

9 How many of the children would suffer from the disease?

_____

_____

Hint 9

✔ *Hints and answers follow*

Genetics

Hints

1. How are body cells and gametes different in the number of chromosomes that they contain?

2. Diploid cells contain a full set of chromosomes. Sperm and egg cells have half the number of chromosomes and have a different word to describe them.

3. If the sperm and egg cells had the same number of chromosomes as the body cells, when fertilisation occurred what would happen to the number of chromosomes in the child compared with the parent?

4. The gene for blue eye colour is recessive, so an individual with blue eyes can only have one possible genotype.

5. In an individual who shows a characteristic produced by a dominant gene, out of the pair of alleles only one needs to be the dominant gene.

6. Use your thinking from question 5 to explain how a dominant characteristic phenotype can have two different genotypes.

7. Using genetic diagrams we showed that there was a 50% chance of any baby being male or female. Will the sex of the next baby be affected by the fact that four out of the six children are female?

8. What must be the genotype of an individual who is suffering from a disease produced by a recessive gene?

9. As with all genetic questions, you should approach this in steps. You should already know the genotype for a sufferer of the disease, next work out the genotype for all the children. Then the number of children with the disease can be counted.

Answers

1 parents' body cells 46 / gamete cells 23 / child's body cells 46 2 haploid 3 to avoid doubling of chromosome number in each generation (fertilisation between two haploid gametes restores diploid number) 4 bb 5 BB / Bb 6 both have brown eyes and gene for brown eyes is dominant, genotype can be BB or Bb, same phenotype 7 no – always 50% chance male or female 8 no – need to have two recessive genes 9 – Colin, Tracy, Lucie – all homozygous recessive

53

Classification, adaptation and evolution

Test your knowledge

10 minutes

1 <u>Classification</u> is when organisms are put into groups according to their features. The five main groups are called <u>Kingdoms</u> .

2 An <u>invertebrate</u> is an animal without a backbone whereas a <u>Vertebrate</u> is an animal with a backbone.

3 A jellyfish is an example of a _____ because it has a hollow body, tentacles and _____ cells.

4 A reptile has _____ , _____ skin and lays eggs.

5 Flowering plants can be divided into _____ and dicotyledons.

6 An organism is _____ to its environment, when it changes to increase its chance of survival.

7 _____ is a series of gradual changes over many generations.

8 Organisms that have advantageous variations will increase their chance of survival. These will be selected for and this process is called _____ _____ .

Answers

If you got them all right, skip to page 57

Classification, adaptation and evolution

Improve your knowledge

30 minutes

1 Organisms can be put into groups according to their features and this is called **classification**. There are five main groups called **kingdoms**. They are called animals, plants, protista (single-celled organisms), fungi and bacteria. Viruses are difficult to put into a group because they are both living and non-living.

2 Animals are either **invertebrates** or **vertebrates**. An invertebrate is an animal without a backbone. A vertebrate is an animal with a backbone.

3 The diagram below shows all the different groups of organisms which are invertebrates. Do you recognise the examples?

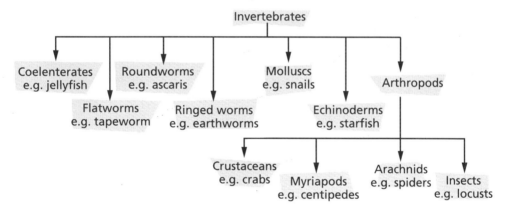

Invertebrates

Coelenterates e.g. jellyfish
Roundworms e.g. ascaris
Molluscs e.g. snails
Arthropods
Flatworms e.g. tapeworm
Ringed worms e.g. earthworms
Echinoderms e.g. starfish
Crustaceans e.g. crabs
Myriapods e.g. centipedes
Arachnids e.g. spiders
Insects e.g. locusts

4 The diagram below shows all the organisms which are vertebrates. Do you recognise the examples?

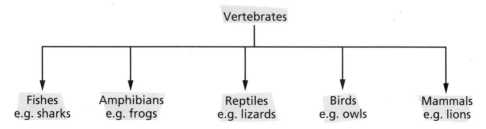

Vertebrates

Fishes e.g. sharks
Amphibians e.g. frogs
Reptiles e.g. lizards
Birds e.g. owls
Mammals e.g. lions

5 There are four main groups of plants. Flowering plants can be divided into two groups called **monocotyledons** and **dicotyledons**.

Group	Feature
Mosses	Small plants with simple leaves and no roots (rhizoids). They reproduce by spores and have no flowers
Ferns	The leaves are called fronds. They also reproduce by spores and have no flowers
Conifers	Trees which have no flowers. They produce cones, e.g. pine trees
Flowering plants	They have flowers and produce seeds inside fruits

6 An organism is **adapted** to its environment, when it changes to increase its chance of survival. Some organisms can change their colour, pattern or shape to become camouflaged in order to avoid being eaten by predators, e.g. lizards.

7 **Evolution** is a series of gradual changes or adaptations over many generations.

8 In each population of organisms, there is great variation within the species due to the inheritance of different genes. Some organisms will have variations that give them a better chance of survival. Variations in organisms which are a disadvantage will be selected against and the number of organisms will decrease, i.e. they will struggle to survive. This process is called **natural selection**. It can lead to evolution or extinction, e.g. peppered moth.

Check list

Are you sure that you understand these key terms?

classification / kingdoms / invertebrates / vertebrates / adaptation / evolution / natural selection

Now learn how to use your knowledge

Classification, adaptation and evolution

Use your knowledge

20 minutes

The diagram shows a penguin swimming through the sea.

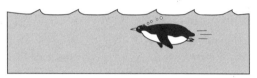

1 Describe two features which show how it is adapted to its environment.

_____

2 Give two ways in which being able to swim quickly helps the penguin survive.

_____

There are two forms of the peppered moth (*Biston betularia*). Before 1850, all the moths found on trees were the light grey peppered moth. However, during the Industrial Revolution, the rare black form of the moth became more common. When the Clean Air Act was passed, the light grey peppered moth began to increase in numbers. These moths are eaten by birds.

3 Why did the numbers of light grey peppered moths decrease during the Industrial Revolution?

_____

4 What happened to the number of black moths during the Industrial Revolution and why?

_____

5 What is this an example of?

_____

✔ *Hints and answers follow*

Classification, adaptation and evolution

1 What is the shape of the body like?

2 What are the wings, feet and tail for?

3 What does it need to eat?

4 What does it need to avoid?

5 Why are the light grey peppered moths more easily seen?

6 What will eat the moths?

7 The Industrial Revolution produced a lot of soot and the trees turned black. Why were the black moths not eaten as much?

8 Learn this – look at number 8 in *Improve your knowledge.*

Answers

1 any of: stream-lined body to glide through the water / strong wings to propel the penguin forward / feet and tail to steer 2 to help catch prey / to avoid predators 3 less camouflaged against surfaces darken by soot and more predation from birds 4 increased: more pollution and the soot settled on the trees, therefore they were better camouflaged 5 natural selection

Health and disease

Test your knowledge

10 minutes

1 Syphilis is a sexually transmitted disease caused by a _bacterium_ .
Micro-organisms which cause diseases and illnesses are called
pathogens .

2 Houseflies cause disease because they carry pathogens from
faeces to human food on their hairy body.

3 Food poisoning is caused by the _contamination_ of food by micro-
organisms. _Salmonella_ is a bacterium that lives in the guts of chicken
that can cause diarrhoea and vomiting if taken in with food.

4 Food can be stopped from going bad by _killing_ the micro-
organisms. For example, _irradiation_ of food using low doses of
X-rays and gamma rays will kill any micro-organisms present.

5 Young children need _more_ protein in their diet than any other
age group, and very active people need more _energy_ .

6 _Obesity_ is a health problem caused by over-eating. People
suffering from anorexia are below normal weight for their height and
age due to _under_ eating.

7 Active people have a slower heart beat rate and greater _lung_
capacity.

Answers

1 bacterium / pathogens 2 faeces/manure/
decaying food 3 contamination / Salmonella
4 killing / irradiation 5 more / energy/
carbohydrate 6 Obesity / under- 7 lung

If you got them all right, skip to page 63

59

Health and disease

Improve your knowledge

1 **Pathogens** are micro-organisms (bacteria and viruses) which cause disease or illness by:

a) Attacking and destroying body cells.

b) Producing poisonous substances (toxins).

Disease	Pathogen	Symptoms	Transmission	Control
Syphilis	Bacterium	Sores and rashes on the body or inside the mouth	Sexual contact. From mother to baby during pregnancy	Antibiotics, e.g. penicillin
Athlete's foot	Fungus	Peeling, blisters and itching between toes and sides of feet	Damp conditions for fungal growth	Anti-fungal creams Foot soaks
Influenza	Virus	Dry cough, sore throat, fever, aching limbs, tiredness	Viruses in airborne water droplets breathed into lungs	Viruses cannot be treated using drugs. Aspirin and cough medicines can reduce symptoms. Vaccines provide protection for several years.

2 This diagram shows an adult housefly.

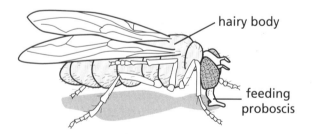

hairy body

feeding proboscis

Houseflies cause disease in several ways:

■ Feeding on dung and decaying food and then feeding on human food transfers harmful pathogens via their hairy bodies.

- To feed, flies place their mouth part (**proboscis**) on the food and pump saliva onto it. They then suck up the digested food as a liquid. This may transfer pathogens onto clean food.
- Faeces produced as they are feeding contains pathogens.

3 Food goes bad (spoiled) when it is **contaminated** (covered) by micro-organisms which feed on the food.

Contamination by micro-organisms can lead to food poisoning, e.g. milk, eggs or meat contaminated with the bacterium **salmonella** can cause diarrhoea and vomiting. These bacteria live in the guts of cattle, pigs and chickens and contamination can occur at farms.

4 **Hygienic food practices** prevent contamination. These include washing hands before handling food, keeping cooked and uncooked food separate and thorough cooking of food.

Technique	Method
Deep-freezing	Food is frozen between −24°C and −18°C. This does not kill micro-organisms, but stops growth and reproduction
Dehydration	Water is removed by blowing hot air over food. This stops enzymes working and micro-organisms become completely inactive. Dried food will last an extremely long time
Vacuum packing	Food is packaged without air. Many microbes cannot survive without oxygen
Irradiation	Sealed food is exposed to low doses of X-rays and gamma rays killing any micro-organisms. Irradiation kills bacteria, such as salmonella, but leaves behind toxins that cause food poisoning

5 A balanced diet will vary for different people at different times of their life:

Age – Young children need more food in proportion to their body weight than adults, particularly protein to make new tissue. Adolescents (12–17 years old) need more calcium than other age groups.

Gender – Females need less protein than males. A pregnant woman needs to increase energy and protein intake slightly and double calcium intake. During lactation (production of breast milk for feeding the baby) energy and protein intake must increase even more.

Activity – Active people need more energy than less active (sedentary) people. For example, an office worker only needs about three-quarters of the energy of a building site worker.

6 An incorrect, or unbalanced diet can lead to a variety of health problems.

Obesity (being overweight) and **high blood pressure** can be caused by over-eating, particularly of fatty or sugary foods. Eating more food than the body needs means the excess is stored as body fat. Obesity and high blood pressure cause heart disease, diabetes and some forms of cancer.

Anorexia is an eating disorder of under-eating. Sufferers are well below the normal weight for their height and age, with problems such as weak bones and muscles, vomiting, kidney damage and sometimes death. The causes are probably psychological, including depression and social pressure to be thin.

7 Regular exercise can produce many benefits to the body:

a) Heart rate goes down.

b) Lung capacity increases (so more oxygen can be taken in at each breath).

c) Muscles used grow larger, with improved appearance or tone.

d) Ligaments and tendons become stronger and more flexible.

e) Psychological 'well-being'. People say that exercise makes them 'feel good'.

Check list

Are you sure that you understand the following key terms?

pathogens / syphilis / athlete's foot / influenza / proboscis / contaminated / food poisoning / salmonella / balanced diet / obesity / anorexia / benefits of exercise

Now learn how to use your knowledge

Health and disease

Use your knowledge

20 minutes

1 What is meant by the term pathogen?

_____ disease causing micro organism _____

2 Syphilis can be passed between people during sexual contact. How else can syphilis be passed on?

Hint 1

_____ Mother →baby during pregnancy. _____

3 Explain why a person coughing without covering their mouth may give you a contagious disease, e.g. influenza.

Hint 2

_____ By coughing you spread the virus out _____
_____ increasing the chance of someone catching _____
it.

Someone suffering from syphilis can be treated with antibiotics (chemicals used to kill bacteria). But someone with the symptoms of influenza cannot be treated with antibiotics.

4 One of the techniques to fight influenza is the use of vaccines. What is the role of influenza vaccines?

Hint 3

_____

5 Explain why antibiotics cannot be used to treat influenza but can be used to treat syphilis.

Hint 4

_____

The list below shows five widely used techniques to prevent food spoilage:

a) Refrigeration. c) Vacuum packing. e) Dehydration.
b) Deep-freezing. d) Irradiation.

6 From the above list, identify two techniques which reduce food spoilage by limiting microbial activity.

Hint 5

_____

7 Explain why a lasagne in a refrigerator will go bad faster than a lasagne in a freezer.

Hint 6

_____

_____

8 Describe how irradiation prevents food spoilage.

_____

_____

To be healthy requires a balanced diet and regular exercise.

9 Explain why over-eating may result in ill health.

Hints 7/8

_____

_____

10 Why is it suggested that adolescents should drink milk?

_____

11 What possible health benefits might help to persuade an inactive person that it would be a good idea for them to start doing some exercise, such as by cycling to work?

Hints 9/10

_____

_____

✓ *Hints and answers follow*

Health and disease

Hints

1   Think about what would happen if a pregnant woman was infected by the syphilis bacterium.

2   In what way is influenza transmitted from sufferers to healthy people?

3   Remember vaccines are given to healthy people.

4   Think about what an antibiotic does and then think about what type of pathogen causes influenza.

5   You must learn about food preservation techniques. See *Improve your knowledge*.

6   Look at number 4 in *Improve your knowledge*.

7   What happens to excess food taken into the body?

8   What are the consequences of obesity?

9   What are the health problems of being inactive?

10   What health benefits are there in regular exercise?

Answers

1 disease-causing micro-organism 2 mother to baby during pregnancy 3 influenza is an airborne virus, coughing and sneezing by sufferer sends viruses into air, greater chance of inhaling virus 4 provides protection against influenza for several years 5 syphilis caused by a bacterium which is killed by antibiotics, influenza is caused by a virus, viruses cannot be killed by antibiotics 6 refrigeration / deep-freezing 7 refrigerator at higher temperature, micro-organisms more active, spoilage occurs quicker 8 sealed food package given low doses of X-rays/gamma rays to kill microbes 9 excess food cannot be utilised, stored around the body as fat, results in high blood pressure, heart problems 10 need large doses of calcium for bone development 11 reduced heart rate, increased lung capacity, greater muscle size and tone, more O_2 carried in blood

Plants and photosynthesis

 *Test your knowledge*

10
minutes

1 Photosynthesis is the process where a plant uses _____ energy to change carbon dioxide and water into _____ and oxygen.

2 The stomata are the _____ which allow gases in and out of the leaf.

3 Factors like light intensity, carbon dioxide and temperature are said to be _____ because they stop the rate of photosynthesis increasing.

4 Plants photosynthesise during the _____ .

5 Glucose is changed into starch, which is stored in _____ _____ .

6 The two transport tissues are called _____ and phloem.

7 _____ is the loss of water from the surface of the leaf by evaporation.

8 A plant which lacks nitrogen has _____ growth and _____ leaves.

9 A plant grows in response to a stimulus and this is called a _____ .

Answers

9 tropism
7 Transpiration 8 stunted / yellow
4 day 5 storage organs 6 xylem
1 solar / glucose/starch 2 pores 3 limiting

 If you got them all right, skip to page 70

66

Plants and photosynthesis

30 minutes

1 **Photosynthesis** is the process where a plant changes solar energy into chemical energy.

Learn the following word equation for photosynthesis:

light energy trapped

carbon dioxide + water ⟶ starch + oxygen

by chlorophyll

2 The structure of the leaf is adapted for photosynthesis. It is thin and flat so it has a large surface area to absorb sunlight and allow for gaseous exchange. Learn to label the cross-section of a leaf:

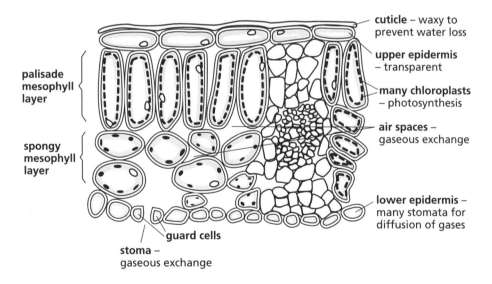

palisade mesophyll layer

spongy mesophyll layer

cuticle – waxy to prevent water loss

upper epidermis – transparent

many chloroplasts – photosynthesis

air spaces – gaseous exchange

lower epidermis – many stomata for diffusion of gases

guard cells

stoma – gaseous exchange

3 The rate of photosynthesis can be increased by increasing the carbon dioxide concentration, light intensity and temperature. However, it only increases up to a maximum level because another factor slows the process. This factor is called a **limiting factor**.

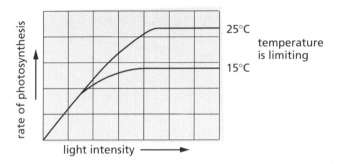

4 Plants respire to release energy from food. This happens both during the day and at night. Photosynthesis happens during the day.

5 Glucose can be:
a) used for respiration to release energy
b) built up into cellulose for new cell walls
c) built into proteins for healthy growth
d) transported to storage organs and converted to starch.

The starch is:
a) stored in storage organs or leaves
b) insoluble (it does not dissolve in water)
c) changed back into glucose.

6 Water and dissolved minerals enter the plant by the root hairs and travel up the microscopic tubes called **xylem** to the leaves. Water is used for photosynthesis and also gives the plant strength to stand upright. The **phloem** carries sugar (made by photosynthesis) to the growing parts of the plant or it is stored as starch.

Cross-section through a stem   Cross-section through a root

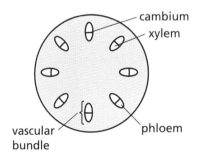

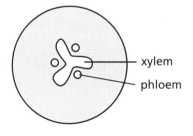

7 **Transpiration** is the loss of water from the leaves by evaporation and through the stomata by diffusion. The rate of water loss can be measured using a **potometer**.

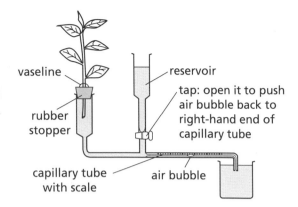

Factors which affect the rate of transpiration are:

a) **Wind** – more wind, faster rate of transpiration.

b) **Humidity** – more humidity, slower rate of transpiration.

c) **Temperature** – higher temperature, faster rate of transpiration.

8 A plant needs **mineral ions** to stay healthy.

Mineral ion	Function	Effect if it is absent
Nitrogen	Forms part of proteins	Stunted growth; yellowing of leaves
Magnesium	Forms chlorophyll	Yellowing of leaves
Potassium	Making proteins; part of enzyme	Yellowing on edges of leaves

9 Plants can detect changes in their environment (stimuli) and respond to them. This growth is called a **tropism**. For example:

a) A shoot growing towards light = **positive phototropism**

b) A shoot growing upwards = **negative geotropism**.

Check list

Are you sure that you understand these key terms?

photosynthesis / limiting factor / xylem / phloem / transpiration / mineral ions / tropism

✔ *Now learn how to use your knowledge*

Plants and photosynthesis

20 minutes

This diagram shows the cross-section of a leaf.

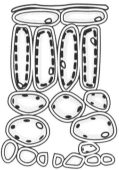

1 In which cells does photosynthesis occur at the fastest rate?

Hints 1/2

_____

2 Explain how these cells are adapted for photosynthesis.

Hints 3/4

_____

_____

3 Look at the diagram of the leaf and explain how it is suited for gaseous exchange.

Hints 5/6

_____

_____

An experiment was carried out to show gaseous exchange in leaves. The test tubes were set up as below and were left in sunlight for 5 days:

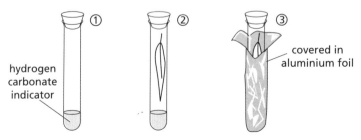

①   ②   ③

hydrogen carbonate indicator

covered in aluminium foil

Hydrogen carbonate indicator changes colour with different pHs.

- It is orange in neutral (pH 7)
- It is yellow in acid (pH below 7)
- It is red/purple in alkali (pH above 7)
- Carbon dioxide is an acidic gas and oxygen is neutral.

The results are shown below

Tube	Colour of indicator
1	Orange
2	Purple/red
3	Yellow

4 What changes in pH have happened in tubes 1 to 3?

Hint 7

_____

_____

5 Explain what has happened in tube 2 to make the indicator turn purple/red?

Hints 8/9

_____

_____

_____

6 Explain what has happened in tube 3 to make the indicator turn yellow?

Hints 10/11/12

_____

_____

_____

7 What was tube 1 set up for and why?

Hints 13/14

_____

_____

_____

Hints and answers follow

Plants and photosynthesis

Hints

1   Which cells are near the surface of the leaf?

2   Which cells contain many chloroplasts for photosynthesis?

3   What do palisade mesophyll cells contain for photosynthesis?

4   Why are they found near the surface of the leaf?

5   What parts of the leaf are involved in gaseous exchange?

6   Look at number 2 in *Improve your knowledge*.

7   What colour has the indicator turned? Use the information given to decide if the pH is neutral, acidic or alkaline.

8   Which gas has been used up from the air in daylight?

9   The leaf is photosynthesising; which gas is used for this process?

10   Tube 3 is in darkness, therefore no photosynthesis can occur.

11   What process occurs during the day and night?

12   Look at number 4 in *Improve your knowledge*.

13   What acidic gas is produced by respiration?

14   What is the test tube called that is set up as a comparison of results?

Answers

1 palisade mesophyll cells **2** many chloroplasts containing chlorophyll to trap sunlight and near surface of leaf for maximum light absorption **3** large air spaces in spongy mesophyll layer and many stomata on lower epidermis **4** tube 1 – no change / tube 2 – increase in pH / tube 3 – decrease in pH **5** the leaf has been in the sunlight and photosynthesising, it has used up the carbon dioxide in the air for photosynthesis, which has led to an increase in pH **6** the leaf has been in the dark, therefore no photosynthesis has occurred, it has only been respiring and has produced carbon dioxide, this has made the solution turn acid to change the indicator to a yellow colour **7** tube 1 was set up as a control to compare results and see if any other factor had changed the colour of the indicator solution

Food chains and webs

Test your knowledge

10 minutes

1 The ultimate source of energy on the Earth is the _Sun_ .
Solar energy is converted into chemical energy by green plants during _photosynthesis_

2 In a food chain the direction of the arrows show the transfer of _energy_ .

3 A _food_ _web_ is a series of inter-connected food chains.

4 The pyramid of numbers shows the number of organisms at each _trophic_ _level_ or feeding level.

5 The pyramid of biomass shows the _mass_ of organisms at each trophic level.

6 Biomass decreases at each level because _energy_ is lost at each level in faeces, urine and as _heat_ during respiration. The greatest biomass is therefore found at trophic level _one_ .

7 Decomposition is the breakdown of dead plant and animal material by organisms such as _bacteria_ and _fungi_ . Decomposition is fastest in _warm_ and wet conditions.

Answers

If you got them all right, skip to page 76

Food chains and webs

30 minutes

1 In any **ecosystem**, solar energy is converted into chemical energy by green plants during photosynthesis. These green plants are known as **producers**. Producers are eaten by herbivores or **primary consumers**, which in turn may be eaten by carnivores (**secondary consumers**). This relationship is shown in a **food chain**.

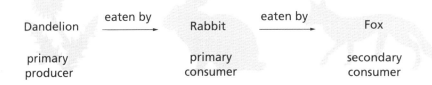

Dandelion	eaten by →	Rabbit	eaten by →	Fox
primary producer		primary consumer		secondary consumer

2 The arrows show the **direction** of energy transfer.

3 Food chains only show part of the picture: foxes eat more than just rabbits and rabbits do not just eat dandelions. A more realistic picture is given in a **food web**.

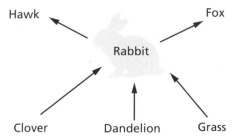

The organisms in the food chain or web can be organised into different feeding or **trophic levels**.

4 The total number of organisms at each trophic level can be shown in a **pyramid of numbers**. The size of the boxes is proportional to the total number of organisms at each level.

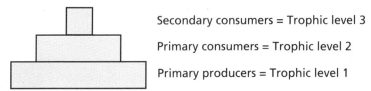

Secondary consumers = Trophic level 3

Primary consumers = Trophic level 2

Primary producers = Trophic level 1

However, imagine the pyramid of numbers based on an oak tree.

Pyramid of numbers based on an oak tree

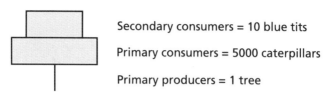

Secondary consumers = 10 blue tits

Primary consumers = 5000 caterpillars

Primary producers = 1 tree

The pyramid is upside down! To get round this we draw a pyramid of biomass.

5 A **pyramid of biomass** shows the mass of all the organisms at each trophic level. The pyramid is the right way up because the tree has a much greater mass than thousands of caterpillars.

Pyramid of numbers based on an oak tree

10 blue tits

5000 caterpillars   mass decreases

1 tree

6 Biomass decreases at each trophic level because there is less energy available at each level. Energy is lost because:

a) The caterpillars only eat a tiny amount of the oak tree.

b) The caterpillars produce faeces which the blue tits do not eat.

c) The oak tree and caterpillars respire and some energy is lost as heat.

7 When plants and animals die their tissues are broken down or decomposed by bacteria and fungi. **Decomposition** is fastest in warm and wet conditions.

Check list

Are you sure that you understand these key terms?

ecosystem / food chain / food web / trophic level / pyramid of numbers / pyramid of biomass / decomposition

 Now learn how to use your knowledge

Food chains and webs

20 minutes

The diagram shows
a food web
in a woodland.

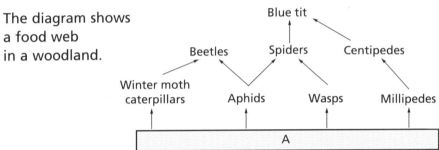

1 Name the source of energy in the food web.

Sun

Hint 1

2 What type of organisms would be in box A?

Primary producers

Hint 2

3 Name a secondary consumer in the food web.

Beetle

Hint 3

4 Which trophic level would have the least biomass?
Explain your answer.

bluetit - lost energy

Hints 4/5

5 Suggest why nutrient recycling is faster in tropical rain
forests than in a woodland in Britain.

Hints 6/7

✓ *Hints and answers follow*

76

Food chains and webs

Hints

1 Learn this!

2 These organisms convert solar energy into the chemical energy which herbivores can use.

3 Learn this.

4 What happens to the amount of energy available at each trophic level?

5 What happens to the energy which is not passed up the food web?

6 What factors affect the rate of decomposition?

7 What do you know about the climate of the two areas?

Answers

1 Sun 2 primary producers/green plants 3 beetle, spider or centipede 4 blue tits or tertiary consumers, because energy is lost between each stage 5 it is warmer and wetter in the rainforest, therefore decomposition is faster

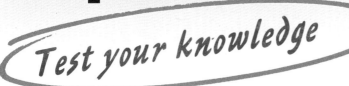

Population

Test your knowledge

10 minutes

1 Complete the box below:

Term	Definition
Population	*amount of people*
Habitat.	The place where a community lives

2 The colour and markings of many animals means that they blend in with their surroundings, i.e. they are well *camoflauged*

3 Plants compete with each other for *heat* , light and nutrients. Animals may compete with each other for *food* , mates and territory.

4 Competition leads to the survival of the *best.* .

5 Predators kill and eat their *prey* . If too many prey are eaten the predators may *starve* and their population will *decrease*

6 As human population increases more *fossil* fuels are burned to provide *heat* for homes, industry and transport.

7 Burning coal in power stations releases *carbon* *dioxide* and *sulphr* *dioxide* .

8 Fresh water habitats such as a stream may be damaged if fertilisers such as *nitrates* are washed in from farmers' fields.

If you got them all right, skip to page 82

Population

Improve your knowledge

30 minutes

1. Learn the following definitions:

Term	Definition
Population	All members of a species, e.g. rabbits living in a particular area at the same time
Community	All the different populations of organisms which live together e.g. grass, plants, dandelions, rabbits, foxes
Habitat	The place where a community lives, e.g. a meadow
Environment	The conditions which exist in a habitat

2. Animals and plants show **adaptations** to their environment which increase their chances of survival. **Camouflage** may allow a predator to sneak up on prey, or it may allow prey to avoid detection by a predator.

3. Animals of the same species and those of different species **compete** with each other for food and territories. Plants compete with each other for nutrients, water and light.

4. Competition means that there are winners and losers. Within a fox population, there will be competition for food such as rabbits. The fastest fox will catch many more rabbits than the slowest fox, which may then starve to death. Competition leads to the **survival of the fittest**.

5. Animals which try to attack and kill other animals are known as **predators**. The animal which is eaten is the **prey**. A large prey population will provide food for many predators whose population also increases. These predators will then eat more food so the prey populations will fall. This means there will be less for predators to eat and some will starve. Less predation allows the prey populations to increase again.

6 Environmental problems have increased as human population has increased. The greater the population, the more energy is required for transport, heating, lighting and industry. This energy is usually obtained by burning more fossil fuels. Food production must also increase – so more fertilisers are used, hedgerows (valuable habitats) are removed and humans over exploit natural resources such as fisheries. Air and water pollution have dramatically increased.

7 Human activity has therefore caused severe **air pollution** . . .

Substance	Source	Effect
Sulphur dioxide	Power stations burning fossil fuels	Dissolves in moisture to form acid rain
Nitrogen dioxide	Vehicle exhaust fumes	Dissolves in moisture to form acid rain
Carbon monoxide	Incomplete combustion of petrol	Odourless, invisible, poisonous gas
CFCs (chloro-fluorocarbons)	Aerosols, refrigeration, foam products	Destroys ozone layer, increasing chances of skin cancer
Carbon dioxide	Power stations burning fossil fuels	Greenhouse effect

8 . . . and **water pollution**.

Substance	Source	Effect
Sewage	Sewage plant floods, e.g. in heavy rainfall	May contain metals, e.g. copper. Will contain pathogenic (disease-causing) bacteria
Nitrates	Dissolved nitrate fertilisers which drain from agricultural land	Leads to algal blooms which are quickly broken down by bacteria. These bacteria use up oxygen in the water, killing fish
Phosphates	Erode from agricultural land	As with nitrates, phosphates encourage algal blooms

Check list

Are you sure that you understand the following key terms?

population / adaptation / camouflage / compete / 'survival of the fittest' / predators / air pollution / water pollution

 Now learn how to use your knowledge

Population

Use your knowledge

The graph shows the population of mice and goshawks in a coniferous wood. The goshawks, which eat mice, rabbits and small birds first arrived in the wood in 1990. The mice eat seeds and buds.

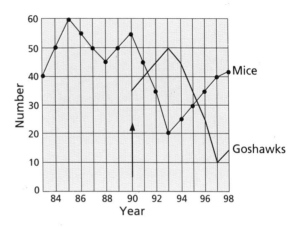

1 In this example, which species is the predator and which is the prey? *(Hint 1)*
_____

2 Suggest reasons why the mouse population went up and down before the goshawks arrived in the wood. *(Hint 2)*
_____
_____

3 Suggest an explanation for the change in the population of the organisms between 1990 and 1992. *(Hints 3/4/5)*
_____
_____

4 If nitrates accidentally enter a pond, the amount of oxygen in the pond may increase initially and then fall dramatically. Explain why this may happen. *(Hints 6/7)*
_____
_____

✓ *Hints and answers follow*

81

Population

Hints

1 Learn the definitions.

2 What factors influence the size of the population?

3 What happened to the goshawk population in 1990–1?

4 What happened to the mouse population over that period?

5 Think 'predator-prey'. How does one population affect the other?

6 Which organisms in the pond will use nitrates?

7 What do you think happens to these organisms when they die?

Mock exam

2 hours

1 a) Complete the table below using a ✔ or a ✘.

Red blood cell   Palisade mesophyll cell   Sperm cell

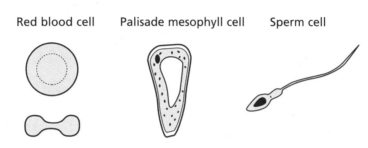

	Red blood cell	Palisade mesophyll cell	Sperm cell
i) Has a tail			✔
ii) Contains chloroplasts		✔	
iii) No nucleus	✔		
iv) Has a cellulose cell wall		✔	
v) Carries oxygen around the body	✔		
vi) Has a cell membrane			
vii) Has a vacuole	✔	✔	✔

(7)

b) In which organ is the palisade mesophyll cell found?

_____ **(1)**

c) Which organ makes sperm cells? _testes._____ **(1)**

d) What is the function of the chloroplast? _____ **(1)**

[10]

2 a) In humans, male cells have two sex chromosomes, XY, and female cells have two sex chromosomes, XX. Using a genetic diagram show how there is a 50% chance of a baby being male, and a 50% chance of a baby being female. **(4)**

Genes are found on chromosomes, which are made up of the organic molecule DNA. DNA can be taken out of cells and separated into bands which give a print of a cell's genetic makeup. This is known as genetic fingerprinting.

A DNA fingerprint from the chromosomes of a cell

Everyone has a unique genetic fingerprint, except identical twins.

b) In which part of the cell are chromosomes found?_____ **(1)**

c) Suggest why even though they have exactly the same genotype 'identical' twins may have differences in appearance or phenotype.

_____

_____ **(3)**

d) Does a male child have a different DNA fingerprint from his father? Explain your answer.

Yes - everybody has different, individual fingerprints

_____ **(3)**

[11]

3 The diagram below shows red blood cells within a capillary blood vessel.

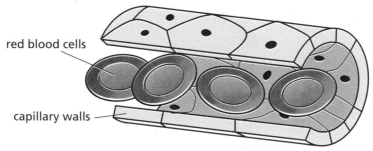

a) What is the main function of red blood cells? <u>Carry O₂ round the</u> **(1)**
<u>body.</u>

b) i) Where in the circulatory system would you expect to find
a capillary vessel? _____

_____ **(1)**

ii) Identify two characteristics of a capillary and explain how each
feature enables the capillary to perform its function.

_____

_____ **(4)**

If a person's number of heartbeats per minute and blood pressure are
measured before, during and after exercise, such as riding a bike, they
will both be seen to increase.

c) i) Give two reasons why heart rate needs to increase during exercise.
_____ **(2)**

ii) What will happen to the person's heart rate if they train
for several weeks? <u>It will increase less when</u>
<u>exercising.</u> **(1)**

d) Identify two advantages, apart from a change in heart rate,
of regular exercise. _____

_____ **(2)**

e) Excluding exercise, suggest one other activity that can cause an increase
in blood pressure. _____

_____ **(1)**

[12]

4 The symptoms of two patients are shown below:

Patient A	Patient B
Vomiting	Aching limbs
Diarrhoea	Headache
Sore throat	Cough

Patient A's symptoms rapidly appeared approximately 6 hours after eating chicken meat. Patient B has been feeling steadily worse for the last week.

a) i) Suggest which diseases patient A and patient B are suffering from.

A = Salmonella (food poisoning) **(2)**
B = flu.

ii) Identify one other symptom which both patients may suffer from.

A - **(1)**
B - meningitis

b) Which type of pathogen may have caused patient A's disease?

_____ **(1)**

c) i) Explain why irradiation of the chicken meat may have stopped patient A becoming ill.

Salmonella lives in a chicken's guts, **(2)**

ii) How can irradiated food still cause food poisoning?

If other food has been in contact in it. **(2)**

d) Suggest one way that patient B may have caught the disease.

Close contact with somebody. **(1)**

e) i) Explain why doctors cannot use antibiotics to treat patient B.

Antibiotics don't help viruses which flu is. **(3)**

ii) Suggest two possible treatments for patient B.

Paracetamol (pain killer)
Rest. **(2)**

[14]

86

5 The table below shows some of the dietary needs of a male during his life up to the age of 35.

Daily needs			
Age	Energy (mJ)	Protein (g)	Calcium (mg)
6 months	4.1	25.0	750
5 years	9.4	56.3	625
15 years	12.0	87.5	875
35 years	11.5	68.8	625

a) i)   What is the role of protein in the body?

_____ **(1)**

   ii) Describe and explain the daily needs of protein up to the age of 35.

His needed more tumore until teen years then needed **(4)**
less.

   iii) Identify two symptoms of a lack of protein in the diet.

_____ **(2)**

b) i)   Starch is a good source of energy in the diet.
        Which food group does starch belong to?

_____ **(1)**

   ii) Name two types of food which are good sources of starch.

Potatoes, rice. **(2)**

   iii) Identify the enzyme that digests starch in humans and name one site in the digestive system where it is produced.

lipase **(2)**

c) Explain why the largest amount of calcium is needed at age 15.

Bones are weaker at that age + calcium strengthens **(2)**
bones.

d) i)   Vitamin C is another essential component of diet.
        Name one good source of vitamin C.

Oranges / citrus fruits. **(1)**

   ii) State two reasons why vitamin C is vital for a healthy body.

_____ **(2)**

[17]

6 The diagram below shows the bones and some of the muscles of the human arm.

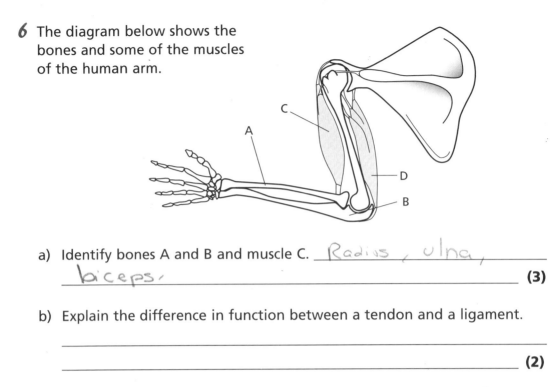

a) Identify bones A and B and muscle C. <u>Radius , ulna,</u>
   <u>biceps.</u>   **(3)**

b) Explain the difference in function between a tendon and a ligament.

   _____
   _____ **(2)**

c) i) Which muscle, C or D, is responsible for flexing the arm? <u>C</u> **(1)**

   ii) Muscles C and D are said to be antagonistic. Explain the meaning
       of this term with regard to the movement of the arm.
       <u>Antagonistic Muscles work in pairs, one does the</u>
       <u>opposite to the other - eg- relax and</u> **(3)**
       <u>contract.</u>

                                                                           [9]

7 The diagram shows a bell jar which represents parts of the thorax.

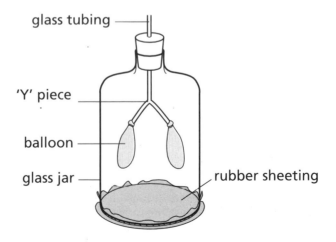

glass tubing

'Y' piece

balloon

glass jar

rubber sheeting

a) Write down what the following parts represent:

    i)   balloon   _lungs_   **(1)**

    ii) glass jar   **(1)**

    iii) rubber sheet _diaphragm_   **(1)**

    iv) glass tube ~~trace~~ _trachea_ **(1)**

    v) 'Y' piece   **(1)**

b) Which parts work in the same way as the thorax?

    (2)

c) Which part works in a different way?

    (1)

d) Explain how air gets into the thorax.

    (3)

    [11]

8 The diagram below shows the development of a human embryo in the uterus of the mother.

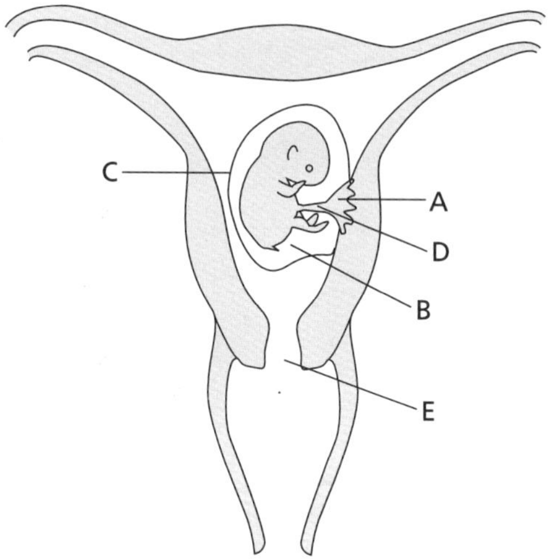

a) Label parts A to E.   **(5)**

b) What is the function of the amniotic fluid?

    (1)

c) Give two functions of the umbilical cord.

    (2)

d) Give two functions of the placenta.

_____ **(2)**

e) How long is the gestation period for a human embryo?

_____ **(1)**

[11]

9 The following experiment is used to show the effect of light intensity on the rate of photosynthesis.

piece of pond weed

folded piece of lead

lamp

a) What variables need to be controlled in this experiment?

__heat, other light sources._____ **(4)**

b) How would the rate of photosynthesis be measured?

__Count bubbles of CO_2 given out in 1 minute._____ **(1)**

c) i) What errors can occur during the experiment?

__Bubbles counted wrongly_____ **(2)**

ii) How would these errors be reduced?

_____ **(2)**

d) Why was the folded piece of lead used?

_____ **(1)**

e) Complete the word equation for photosynthesis given below:

_____ + _____ $\xrightarrow[\text{chlorophyll}]{\text{sunlight}}$ _____ + _____ **(2)**

f) What two other factors limit the rate of photosynthesis?

_____ **(2)**

[14]

10 The diagram below shows decaying rubbish.

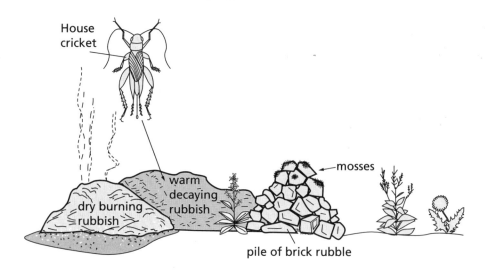

a) Name two types of organisms which cause decay.

_____ **(2)**

b) What two conditions are needed for decay?

_____ **(2)**

c) What group of animals do house crickets belong to?

_____ **(1)**

d) What external features helped you decide which group they belong to?

___Backbone, amount of legs._____ **(2)**

e) What type of pollution will be caused by burning the rubbish?

___CO₂_____ **(1)**

[8]

Total marks for paper = 117

Answers

1 a)

	Red blood cell	Palisade mesophyll cell	Sperm cell
i) Has a tail	✗	✗	✔
ii) Contains chloroplasts	✗	✔	✗
iii) No nucleus	✔	✗	✗
iv) Has a cellulose cell wall	✗	✔	✗
v) Carries oxygen around the body	✔	✗	✗
vi) Has a cell membrane	✔	✔	✔
vii) Has a vacuole	✗	✔	✗

b) Leaf.
c) Testis.
d) To trap light for photosynthesis.

2 a) See genetic diagram in *Improve your knowledge*, page 50.
b) Nucleus.
c) Characteristics are controlled by environment, as well as genes. Therefore, twins in different environments will show differences in appearance.
d) Yes, child's genetic makeup is 50% from the father and 50% from the mother.

3 a) Transport of oxygen.
b) i) Linking arteries to veins / in close association with body cells.
 ii) One cell thick – allow rapid diffusion between blood and body cells; pores – allow plasma, white blood cells and platelets to move around cells; close association with cells – allow all cells to exchange useful material and waste with the blood.
c) i) Deliver more O_2; remove more CO_2 from active muscles; pick up more O_2 from lungs; remove more CO_2 at lungs.
 ii) Decrease.
d) Heartbeat rate goes down; lung capacity increases, blood carries more oxygen; muscle size and tone increase; ligaments and tendons become stronger/more flexible; psychological 'well-being'.
e) Over-eating (of fatty foods).

4 a) i) A – (salmonella) food poisoning; B – influenza. ii) Fever.
  b) (Salmonella) bacteria
  c) i) Low doses of gamma radiation will destroy bacteria and micro-organisms.
     ii) Radiation kills bacteria but toxins produced may remain and cause food poisoning.
  d) Breathing in viruses in airborne water droplets.
  e) i) Antibiotics work against bacteria, influenza is caused by a virus, so will not be affected by antibiotics.
     ii) Asprin, paracetamol and cough medicines can reduce symptoms; vaccines provide protection; bed rest and drinking large amounts of liquids.

5 a) i) Structural/enzymes/energy source.
     ii) Protein needs increase up until the age of 15, declines to 35 years. Fastest growth occurs up to 15, protein is needed to provide growth.
     iii) Swollen belly, slow growth and slow brain development.
  b) i) Carbohydrate.
     ii) Bread, pasta.
     iii) Amylase; mouth/small intestine from pancreas.
  c) Age of highest growth rate, needed for bone development.
  d) i) Citrus fruit.
     ii) Healthy teeth and gums; healing of wounds.

6 a) A – radius; B – ulna; C – bicep.
  b) Tendon joins muscles to bones; ligament joins bones together.
  c) i) Muscle C.
     ii) Both muscle C and D are needed to move the arm; muscle C flexes; muscle D extends.

7 a) i) Lung.
     ii) Rib cage.
     iii) Diaphragm.
     iv) Trachea.
     v) Bronchi.
  b) Rubber sheet, balloon.
  c) Glass jar.
  d) Diaphragm contracts and flattens, this increases the volume of the thorax, decreasing the pressure and thus air rushes in to equalise the pressure.

8 a) A – placenta; B – amniotic fluid; C – amniotic sac; D – umbilical cord; E – cervix / neck of womb.
  b) To protect the embryo from shock and bumps.
  c) Carries oxygen and food from mother to embryo or carries urea and carbon dioxide from embryo to mother; connects embryo to placenta.
  d) Allows diffusion of food and oxygen from mother's blood to embryo's blood; acts as a barrier between the two blood supplies.
  e) Nine months.

9 a) Same length and piece of pondweed; same temperature of water; same volume of water; same wattage of light bulb; constant concentration of CO_2 in water; constant incident light.

b) Number of bubbles of oxygen produced in the same time/the time it takes for the pondweed to produce 10 bubbles.

c) i) Other sources of light than the light bulb; heat from the light bulb.
ii) Darken the room; use a heat shield.

d) To hold the pondweed down.

e) carbon dioxide + water $\xrightarrow[\text{chlorophyll}]{\text{sunlight}}$ starch + oxygen

f) Carbon dioxide concentration; temperature.

10 a) Bacteria and fungi.

b) Warm and damp.

c) Insects.

d) Six legs; a pair of antennae; body divided into three main parts (head, thorax, abdomen); wings or wing buds.

e) Air pollution by producing carbon dioxide.